Usborne
Essential French Phrases

Nicole Irving, Leslie Colvin and Kate Needham

Illustrated by Ann Johns

Language consultants: Renée Chaspoul, Annick Dunbar, Zina Rahouadj, Lorraine Beurton-Sharp and Pascal Varejka.

Edited by Rachel Firth
Series editor: Sue Meredith
American Editor: Carrie Armstrong

Usborne Quicklinks

The Usborne Quicklinks Website is packed with links to all the best websites on the internet. For links to some great websites to help you learn French, go to **www.usborne-quicklinks.com** and enter the keywords: "essential french"

When using the internet please follow the internet safety guidelines displayed on the Usborne Quicklinks Website.

The recommended websites in Usborne Quicklinks are regularly reviewed and updated, but Usborne Publishing Ltd. is not responsible for the content or availability of any website other than its own. We recommend that children are supervised while using the internet.

Contents

About this book

This book gives simple, up-to-date French to help you survive, travel and socialize in France. It also gives basic information about France and tips for low budget travelers.

Finding the right words

Use the contents list on page 3 to find the section of the book you need. If you don't find a phrase where you expect it to be, try a related section. There are food words, for example, on several pages. If you still can't find the word, try looking it up in the word list at the back.

Go for it

Remember that you can make yourself clear with very few words, or words that are not quite right. Saying "Paris?" while pointing at a train will provoke *oui* or *non* (yes or no). The French listed on the opposite page is absolutely essential.

You will feel more confident if you have some idea of how to pronounce French correctly and of how the language works. If French is new to you, try looking through the sections on pages 55-60. A good pronunciation tip is to make your voice go up at the end of a question. This will help it to sound different from a statement.

Being polite

Words like *excusez-moi* and *pardon* (excuse me), *s'il vous plaît* (please) or *merci* (thank you) make anything sound more polite and will generally guarantee a friendly response.

There are other ways of being polite in French. The words *Monsieur* (Sir) and *Madame* (Madam) are often used to address older people whose names you don't know, ex. *Bonjour, Monsieur* (Hello, Sir) or *Merci, Madame* (Thank you, Madam.)

French has two different words for "you" – *tu* and *vous*. You can use the casual *tu* for a friend, or someone your own age or younger. It is important, though, always to use the polite *vous* when you talk to an older person, whether you know them or not. Saying *tu* to someone who doesn't expect it can be very rude. For more than one person, always use *vous*. In this book *tu* or *vous* is given depending on the situation. Sometimes you will have to judge which is best, so both are given. If you are ever in doubt, say *vous*.

The language in this book is everyday, spoken French, ranging from the formal to the colloquial. An asterisk after a French word shows that it is slang or fairly familiar, ex. *rasoir** (boring). Two asterisks indicate that a word is strong slang and could be considered very impolite.

Masculine or feminine?

Adjectives with two forms in French are given twice, ex. *vert/verte* (green). The first is masculine (m) and the second is feminine (f). You can find out more about masculine and feminine in French on pages 56 and 57.

Excusez-moi, nous sommes perdues.
Excuse me, we're lost.

Vous allez où?
Where are you going?

yes	oui
no	non
maybe	peut-être
I don't know.	Je ne sais pas.
I don't mind.	Ça m'est égal.
please	s'il vous plaît/s'il te plaît
thank you	merci
excuse me	pardon, excusez-moi
sorry	pardon, désolé/désolée
I'm very sorry.	Je suis désolé/désolée.
It's nothing/Don't mention it.	Ce n'est rien.
hello	bonjour
goodbye	au revoir
hi	salut
bye	salut
good morning	bonjour
good evening	bonsoir
good night	bonne nuit
see you soon	à bientôt
Mr., Sir	Monsieur
Mrs., Madam	Madame
and	et
or	ou
when?	quand?
where is?	où est?
why?	pourquoi?
because	parce que
how?	comment?
how much?	combien?
How much is it?	C'est combien?
how many?	combien?
What is it/this?	Qu'est-ce que c'est?/ C'est quoi?
it/this is	c'est
is there?	est-ce qu'il y a?/il y a?
there is	il y a
I'd like	je voudrais
could I have?	je peux avoir?

Getting help with French

I don't understand.
Je ne comprends pas.

Can you write it down?
Vous pouvez me l'écrire?
Tu peux me l'écrire?

Can you say that again?
Vous pouvez répéter?
Tu peux répéter?

A little slower, please.
Un peu plus lentement, s'il vous/te plaît.

What does this word mean?
Que veut dire ce mot?

What's the French for this?
Comment on dit ça en français?

Do you have a dictionary?
Vous avez un dictionnaire?
Tu as un dictionnaire?

Do you speak English?
Vous parlez anglais? Tu parles anglais?

Plus lentement, s'il te plaît.
Slower, please.

Signs you may see

Sortie de secours	**Emergency exit**
Attention	**Beware**
Chien méchant	**Beware of the dog**
Défense d'entrer	**Keep out, no entry**
Interdit de fumer	**No smoking**
Propriété privée	**Private property**
Danger	**Danger**
Eau potable	**Drinking water**
Eau non potable	**Not drinking water**
Baignade interdite	**No swimming**
Camping sauvage interdit	**No unauthorized camping**

Jean est là, s'il vous plaît?
Is John there, please?

Asking the way

Je suis perdu.
I'm lost.

Vous pouvez m'aider, s'il vous plaît?
Can you help me, please?

Où est l'office du tourisme?
Where is the tourist office?

Vous pouvez me dessiner un plan?
Can you draw me a map?

Est-ce qu'il y a des toilettes publiques par ici?
Is there a public toilet around here?

Fact file

Most large towns have an *office du tourisme* (tourist office), sometimes called *syndicat d'initiative*. It's often near the station or town hall. In tourist areas even small towns have one, but opening times may be restricted. Most tourist offices will provide town plans and leaflets on local sights free of charge, and some sell maps and booklets. They also give advice on places to stay and travel arrangements. They often employ someone who speaks English.

Go straight ahead.
Allez tout droit.

Follow the signs for Blois.
Suivez les panneaux pour Blois.

Take the first on the left.
Prenez la première rue à gauche.

Take the second turn on the right.
Prenez le deuxième tournant à droite.

It's on the left/right.
C'est à gauche/à droite.

Go left/right.
Allez à gauche/à droite.

It's...	C'est...
Go...	Allez...
Keep going...	Continuez...
straight ahead	tout droit
Turn...	Tournez...
left, on the left	à gauche
right, on the right	à droite
Take...	Prenez...
the first	le premier/la première
the second	le/la deuxième
the third	le/la troisième
the fourth	le/la quatrième
turning	le tournant
crossroads, junction	le carrefour
traffic circle	le rond-point
traffic lights	les feux
pedestrian crossing	le passage piétons
subway	le passage souterrain
Cross...	Traversez...
Follow...	Suivez...
street	la rue, le boulevard
road	la route
path	le chemin, le sentier
main street	la rue principale
square	la place, le square
highway	l'autoroute
beltway, loop	le boulevard périphérique

one way	sens unique
no entry	sens interdit
no parking	stationnement interdit
parking lot	un parking
parking meters	des parcmètres
pedestrian area	une zone piétonne
pedestrians	piétons
sidewalk	le trottoir
town center	le centre-ville
in town, to town	en ville
area, part of town	le quartier
outskirts, suburbs	la banlieue
town hall	la mairie, l'hôtel de ville
bridge	le pont
river	la rivière
park	le jardin public
post office	la poste
stores, shops	les magasins
church	l'église
school	l'école
museum	le musée
railway line	la ligne de chemin de fer
just before the	juste avant le/la
just after the	juste après le/la
to the end of	jusqu'au bout de
on the corner	au coin
next to	près de
opposite	en face de
in front of	devant
behind	derrière
above	au-dessus, en haut
below	au-dessous, en bas
over	par-dessus
under	en dessous
in	dans
on	sur
here	ici
there	là
over there	là-bas
far	loin
close, near	près (de)
nearby	tout près, juste à côté près
near here	d'ici
around here	dans les alentours, par ici
somewhere	quelque part
in this area	dans ce quartier
10 minutes walk	à dix minutes de marche
5 minutes drive	à cinq minutes en voiture
on foot	à pied

Quel est le meilleur chemin pour aller au camping?
What's the best way to the campsite?

Vous pouvez me montrer sur la carte?
Can you show me on the map?

Où est la plage la plus proche?
Where's the nearest beach?

C'est loin?
How far is it?

Pour aller à l'auberge de jeunesse, s'il vous plaît?
How do I get to the youth hostel?

Travel: trains, subways, buses

Getting information

A quelle heure est le prochain train pour Toulouse?
What time is the next train to Toulouse?

Combien de temps dure le voyage?
How long is the journey?

Je dois changer?
Do I have to change?

Fact file

The *SNCF* (French railways) runs an extensive rail network and operates some bus services. Fares are cheapest during the off-peak *période bleue* (blue period). Before you get on a train, look for the sign *Compostez votre billet* (Stamp your ticket), stamp it in the orange machine, then hang on to it. *TGV* are high speed trains – you reserve in advance and may pay an additional fee. *TER* (*Trans Express Régional*) are the slowest, stopping trains. The under-26 InterRail and Eurail passes are valid throughout the country. The Paris *métro* is easy to use; maps are free from stations. Check the number of the line you want and the direction – the last stop on the line gives you this, ex. *direction Pont de Neuilly*. The same tickets are valid on the *métro*, buses, trams and the central zone of the *RER* (Paris express trains). A book of ten tickets works out cheaper than single tickets. They are available from *tabacs* (tobacco shops) as well as newsstands kiosks and stations. For a book of tickets, ask for *un carnet*.

Je change où pour la gare St-Lazare?
Where do I change for St-Lazare?

Qu'est-ce qu'on vient d'annoncer?
What did they just say over the loudspeaker?

C'est quel quai pour les Halles?
Which platform for Les Halles?

Tickets

Où est-ce que je peux acheter un billet?
Where can I buy a ticket?

Un aller simple pour Avignon, s'il vous plaît.
Can I have a single to Avignon?

J'ai droit à une réduction?
Can I get a reduced fare?

Comment marche cette machine?
How does this machine work?

I'd like to reserve a seat.	Je voudrais réserver une place.	**youth fare**	tarif jeune
railway station	la gare	**ticket (bus/tube)**	un ticket
subway	la station de métro	**ticket (train)**	un billet
bus station	la gare routière	**a single**	un aller simple
bus stop	l'arrêt d'autobus	**a return**	un aller et retour
train	le train	**book of tickets**	un carnet de tickets
subway	le métro	**additional fee**	un supplément
tram	le tramway	**left luggage locker**	le casier de consigne
bus	l'autobus	**track**	la voie
coach	le car	**connection**	une correspondance
leaves at 2 o'clock	part a deux heures	**schedule**	l'horaire
arrives at 4 o'clock	arrive à quatre heures	**arrivals/departures**	arrivées/départs
first/last	le premier/le dernier	**long distance**	grandes lignes
next	le prochain	**local, suburban**	banlieue
cheapest	le moins cher	**every day**	tous les jours
ticket office	le guichet	**weekdays**	semaine
ticket machine	un distributeur automatique	**Sundays and holidays**	dimanches et jours fériés
fare	le tarif	**in the summertime**	pendant l'été
student fare	tarif étudiant	**out of season**	hors saison
		except	sauf

Buses

C'est bien le bus pour Versailles?
Is this the right bus for Versailles?

Où va cet autobus?
Where does this bus go?

Vous pouvez me dire où je dois descendre?
Can you tell me where to get off?

Travel: air, sea, taxis

Je voudrais confirmer mon vol.
I'd like to confirm my flight.

A quelle heure je dois faire enregistrer les bagages?
What time should I check in?

Où est-ce que je fais enregistrer mes bagages?
Where do I check in?

Fact file

Airports and ports usually have signs and announcements in English. There's often a *navette* (bus shuttle) from the airport into town.

Taxis have a standard pick-up charge plus a metered fare; each large bag is charged extra. Taxis often take only three passengers, but they can be good value.

Mes bagages ne sont pas arrivés.
My luggage hasn't arrived.

Madame Duclos est supposée me rencontrer.
Mrs. Duclos is supposed to be meeting me.

Where is the taxi stand?
Où est la station de taxi?

Take me to...
Emmenez-moi à...

What's the fare to... ?
C'est combien pour aller à... ?

Please drop me here.
Laissez-moi ici, s'il vous plaît.

airport	l'aéroport
port	le port
airplane	l'avion
ferry	le ferry
hovercraft	l'aéroglisseur
flight	le vol
the English Channel	la Manche
rough	agité/agitée
calm	calme
I feel sea sick	j'ai le mal de mer
on board	à bord
suitcase	une valise
backpack	un sac à dos
bag	un sac
hand luggage	des bagages à main
baggage cart	un chariot
information	renseignements
customs	la douane
passport	le passeport
departure gate	la porte (de départ)
boarding pass	la carte d'embarquement
foot passenger	passager sans véhicule
travel agent	l'agence de voyages
airline ticket	un billet d'avion
reduced rate	à prix réduit
standby	sans garantie
charter flight	un vol charter
flight number	le numéro de vol
a booking	une réservation
to change	changer
to cancel	annuler
a delay	un retard

Fact file

You can rent bikes from bike shops and some train stations. To find out about taking a bike on a train, see *SNCF* leaflet *Guide du train et du vélo*.

You can ride mopeds from age 14, but must be insured and wear a helmet. Remember the French drive on the right. When you get to a town, follow signs for *Toutes/Autres directions* (all/other directions) until you see the signs you want.

Yield to traffic coming from the right.
Priorité à droite.

Fill it up, please.
Le plein, s'il vous plaît.

I have a puncture.
J'ai crevé.

The engine won't start.
Le moteur ne démarre pas.

The battery's dead.
La batterie est à plat.

How much will it cost?
Ça va coûter combien?

for rent/hire
à louer

Can I rent/hire... ?
Je voudrais louer...

Where are you going?
Tu vas où?/Vous allez où?

I'm going to St-Jean-de-Luz.
Je vais à St-Jean-de-Luz.

Je suis tombé en panne.
I've broken down.

Où est le garage le plus proche?
Where's the nearest garage?

town center	centre-ville
yield	cédez le passage, priorité à droite
toll	le péage
insurance	l'assurance
driver's license	le permis de conduire
(car) registration	les papiers
crash helmet	un casque
gas station	une station-service
gasoline	de l'essence
lead-free gasoline	de l'essence sans plomb
oil/gas mixture	du mélange
garage, repair shop	un garage
oil	de l'huile
liter	un litre
car	une voiture/une bagnole*
bicycle	un vélo
moped	un vélomoteur
motorcycle	une moto
radiator	le radiateur
lights	les phares
chain	la chaîne
wheel	la roue
gears	les vitesses
cable	le câble
pump	la pompe
tire	le pneu
inner tube	la chambre à air

Les freins ne marchent pas.
The brakes don't work.

Je ne sais pas ce qui ne va pas.
I don't know what's wrong.

Vous pouvez réparer ça?
Can you fix it?

Accommodations: places to stay

At the tourist office

Vous avez une liste de campings?
Do you have a list of campsites?

Fact file

The *office du tourisme* or *syndicat d'initiative* (tourist office) will supply lists of places to stay. Cheaper options include *auberges de jeunesse* (youth hostels) - a good idea in towns and cities; *gîtes d'étape* - basic hostels in walking or cycling areas; and *relais routiers* - restaurants with basic rooms. *Chambres d'hôte* is bed and breakfast accommodations in someone's home but this may be no cheaper than a basic hotel.

Camping

Fact file

There are lots of *campings* (campsites). The local *camping municipal* is often the cheapest.

Is there a campsite around here?
Est-ce qu'il y a un camping par ici?

Where are the showers?
Où sont les douches?

tent	une tente
motorhome	une caravane
hot water	l'eau chaude
cold water	l'eau froide
drinking water	l'eau potable
camping gas	une cartouche de camping gaz
tent peg	un piquet
mallet	un maillet
sleeping bag	un sac de couchage
flashlight	une lampe de poche
matches	les allumettes
toilet paper	du papier hygiénique
can opener	un ouvre-boîte

Il y a un emplacement de libre?
Do you have a space?

On est trois avec une tente.
There are three of us with a tent.

Il y a un magasin?
Do you have a store?

On peut boire l'eau du robinet?
Is it OK to drink the tap water?

Hotels

Vous avez une chambre?
Do you have a room?

C'est complet.
We're full.

Vous connaissez un autre hôtel par ici.
Is there another hotel nearby?

Combien coûte la chambre?
How much for a room?

Fact file

Ungraded and 1 and 2 star *hôtels* are the cheapest. Most have rooms for three or four people which cuts costs. *Demi-pension* (half-board) and *pension* (full board) can be good value.

Le petit déjeuner est compris?
Does that include breakfast?

Je peux voir la chambre?
Can I see the room?

Rooms available
Chambres à louer/Chambres d'hôte

There are three of us.
Nous sommes trois.

How many nights?
Combien de nuits?

How much do you want to pay?
Combien vous voulez payer?

Can I leave a message for someone?
Je peux laisser un mot pour quelqu'un?

Can I have my passport back?
Vous pouvez me rendre mon passeport?

one/two night(s)	une/deux nuit(s)
room	une chambre
single	pour une personne
double	pour deux personnes
with three beds	avec trois lits
clean	propre
cheap	pas cher/chère
expensive	cher/chère
lunch	le déjeuner
dinner (evening)	le dîner
key	la clé
room number	le numéro de la chambre
registration form	une fiche

Je cherche une chambre pour deux personnes.
I'm looking for a room for two people.

Vous pouvez me réserver une chambre?
Can you book a room for me?

Accommodations: staying with people

Greetings

Bonjour.
Hello.

Comment ça va?
How are you?

Où est-ce que je peux mettre mes affaires?
Where can I put my things?

Je dors où?
Where am I sleeping?

For more polite or formal greetings, say *Bonjour* followed by *Monsieur* or *Madame*. Also use the polite *vous* form: *Comment allez-vous?* (How are you?) (See page 4.)

A quelle heure est le petit déjeuner?
What time do you have breakfast?

Tu peux me réveiller à sept heures?
Could you wake me up at seven?

Bathing

Comment marche la douche?
How does the shower work?

Is it OK if I take a bath?
Je peux prendre un bain?
Do you mind if I wash a few things?
Je peux laver quelques affaires?
Where can I dry these?
Où est-ce que je peux faire sécher ça?

bathroom	la salle de bain
bathtub	un bain
shower	une douche
toilet	les toilettes, les cabinets
bidet	le bidet
towel	une serviette
soap	du savon
shampoo	du shampooing
toothpaste	du dentifrice
toothbrush	une brosse à dents
deodorant	un déodorant
hairdryer	un sèche-cheveux
hairbrush	une brosse à cheveux
laundry detergent	de la lessive

Being polite

Je peux payer quelque chose?
Can I pay my share?

Non, ne t'inquiète pas.
No, don't worry.

C'est gentil à vous de me recevoir.
It's nice of you to let me stay.

Tout va bien.
Everything's OK.

alarm clock	un réveil
sleeping bag	un sac de couchage
on the floor	par terre
an extra...	un/une autre...
blanket	une couverture
quilt	une couette
sheet	un drap
pillow	un oreiller
bolster†	un traversin
electric socket	une prise
needle	une aiguille
thread	du fil
scissors	des ciseaux
iron	un fer à repasser
upstairs	en haut
downstairs	en bas
cabinet	un placard
bedroom	la chambre
living room	le salon
kitchen	la cuisine
garden, yard	le jardin
balcony	le balcon

I'm tired.
Je suis fatigué/fatiguée.

I'm really exhausted.
Je suis crevé/crevée.

I'm cold.
J'ai froid/froide.

I'm hot.
J'ai chaud/chaude.

Can I have a key?
Je peux avoir une clé?

What is there to do in the evenings?
Qu'est-ce qu'on peut faire le soir?

Where's the nearest pay phone?
Où est la cabine téléphonique la plus proche?

Saying goodbye

Merci pour tout.
Thank you for everything.

Au revoir.
Goodbye.

C'est combien pour appeler l'Angleterre?
How much is it to call Britain?

Je peux utiliser votre téléphone?
Can I use your phone?

Je veux payer la communication.
I'll pay for the call.

For more about making phone calls, see page 17.

†A long tube-shaped pillow sometimes used in France.

Banks

Je voudrais changer de l'argent.
I want to change this.

Vous prenez les traveller's chèques?
Do you accept traveler's checks?

Je peux voir votre passeport?
Can I see your passport?

Post office

Je voudrais un timbre pour envoyer ça.
Can I have a stamp for this?

Pardon, il y a une boîte aux lettres par ici?
Where's the nearest mailbox?

Fact file

The unit of currency is the euro (EUR). 1 euro = 100 eurocents. Most banks are open Monday to Friday 9am to 12 noon and 2pm to 4pm. Some open on Saturday and close on Monday. *Bureaux de change* (foreign exchange offices) are often open outside banking hours but will probably give a poorer rate of exchange.

Money problems

J'ai perdu mes traveller's chèques.
I've lost my traveler's checks.

Les numéros de la série sont...
The serial numbers were...

Comment je fais pour en avoir d'autres?
How do I get replacements?

J'attends de l'argent; il est arrivé?
I'm expecting some money; has it arrived?

bank	une banque	cell phone	un mobile, portable
cashier's desk, register	la caisse	directory	un annuaire
foreign exchange	un bureau de change	phone number	le numéro de téléphone
information	des renseignements	wrong number	le mauvais numéro
money	de l'argent	collect call charge	un appel en PCV
small change	de la monnaie	Hang on.	Ne quittez pas.
bills (paper money)	des billets		
traveler's checks	des traveller's chèques, des chèques de voyage		
credit card	une carte de crédit, une carte bancaire		
exchange rate	le cours du change		
commission	la commission		
money transfer	une mise à disposition		
post office	un bureau de poste		
postcard	une carte postale		
letter	une lettre		
package	un colis		
by airmail	par avion		
by registered mail	en recommandé		
stamp	un timbre		
telephone	un téléphone		
telephone booth	une cabine téléphonique		

The cash machine (ATM) has swallowed my credit card.
Le distributeur (DAB) a avalé ma carte de crédit.

Where can I send an e-mail?
Où est-ce que je peux envoyer un e-mail?

Fact file

Phone booths take *télécartes* (phonecards). You can receive incoming calls if the number is shown in the booth. There are also phones in cafés. These are often metered and you pay after the call. You can buy phonecards from phone stores and *tabacs* (see page 24), and stamps from *tabacs* too as well as post offices. For useful phone numbers see page 49.

Phones

Ce téléphone ne marche pas.
This phone doesn't work.

C'est bien l'indicatif pour la Belgique?
Is this the code for Belgium?

Allô, Sylvie est là, s'il vous plaît?
Hello, is Sylvie there, please?

Dites-lui que j'ai appelé, s'il vous plaît.
Please tell her/him I called.

Elle rentre quand?
When will she be back?

Elle/il peut me rappeler?
Can she/he call me back?

Mon numéro est le...
My number is...

Je peux laisser un message pour...?
Can I leave a message for...?

Cafés

café	un café, un bar, un café-brasserie
at the bar	au comptoir
Cheers!	A ta/votre santé!
something to drink	quelque chose à boire
something to eat	quelque chose à manger
snack	un casse-croûte
black coffee	un café, un express
(large) white coffee	un (grand) crème
decaffeinated	décaféiné, déca
white decaff.	un déca-crème
tea (with milk)	un thé (au lait)
hot chocolate	un chocolat chaud
fruit juice	un jus de fruit
orange juice	un jus d'orange
coke	un coca
still mineral water	de l'eau (minérale) plate
carbonated mineral water	de l'eau gazeuse
beer (bottled)	une bière
beer (draft)	une pression, un demi
bottle of...	une bouteille de...
half a bottle of white wine	une demi-bouteille de vin blanc
glass of red wine	un verre de vin rouge
milk	du lait
sugar	du sucre
ice	avec des glaçons
slice of lemon	une tranche de citron
cheese/ham sandwich	un sandwich au fromage/jambon
omelet (plain)	une omelette (nature)

Fact file

Cafés are open varying hours for drinks, snacks, and meeting up with friends. Prices vary. If you sit down, a waiter serves you. Drinks may be cheaper if you stand at the bar. Tea comes with lemon – ask for milk if you want it. Try *citron pressé* or *orange pressée* (freshly squeezed lemon or orange) – you add your own water and sugar. Snacks include *croque-monsieur* (toasted ham and cheese sandwich).

On prend un café?
How about a cup of coffee?

Cette chaise est libre?
Is this chair free?

Je peux voir la carte?
Can I see the menu?

Un café, s'il vous plaît.
A black coffee, please.

Vous avez des milk-shakes?
Do you have milk shakes?

Eating out

Choosing a place

On va où?
Where shall we go?

Je n'aime pas les pizzas.
I don't like pizzas.

Si on allait manger un hamburger?
What about a hamburger?

French food	la cuisine française	**mixed salad**	une salade composée
Moroccan food	la cuisine marocaine	**green salad**	une salade verte
cheap restaurant	un restaurant pas cher	**spaghetti**	des spaghettis
fast-food	la fast-food	**rare**	saignant
carryout, take-out	à emporter	**medium**	à point
menu	la carte	**well done**	bien cuit
appetizer	l'entrée	**mustard**	la moutarde
main course	le plat principal	**salt**	le sel
dessert	le dessert	**pepper**	le poivre
price	le prix	**dressing**	la vinaigrette
soup	de la soupe, du potage	**mayonnaise**	la mayonnaise
fish	du poisson		
meat	de la viande		
vegetables	des légumes	**Is everything all right?**	
cheese	du fromage	Tout va bien?	
fruit	des fruits	**Yes, it's very good.**	
french fries	des frites	Oui, c'est très bon.	
sausage	des saucisses		

Deciding what to have

Je peux en avoir un sans fromage?
Can I have one without cheese?

C'est quoi, ça?
What's that?

Un comme ça, s'il vous plaît.
One of those please.

Problems

> J'ai demandé un steak frites.
> **I ordered steak and fries.**

> Ce n'est pas assez cuit.
> **This isn't cooked enough.**

> Vous n'avez pas de ketchup?
> **Don't you have any ketchup?**

> S'il vous plaît!
> **Excuse me!**

> L'addition s'il vous plaît.
> **Can we have the bill please?**

> Je n'ai pas commandé ça.
> **I didn't order this.**

Fact file

Standard French dishes are *steak frites* or *poulet frites* (steak and fries or chicken and fries). Try the *specialités régionales* (regional specialities) or *couscous* (a North African dish). Red meat is often served rare. Ask for *très, très cuit* if you want it very well done.

Restaurants are sometimes called brasseries. Look for *le menu, le menu du jour* or *le menu touristique* (set menu) which is displayed outside with its price. It is usually three courses and is cheaper than eating *à la carte*. *Le plat du jour* (dish of the day) is often a good value.

Cafés do snacks and simple meals (see page 18) but they can be pricey. Look for stalls selling *crêpes* (pancakes with various fillings), *galettes* (buckwheat pancakes) and *gaufres* (waffles), and for fast-food places. These should be cheaper.

Somwhere on the bill, it will say *'service compris'* which means the tip is included. This is usually 15% of the total bill. If you really enjoyed the meal, you can leave a small tip in addition to this, but you don't have to.

Best times to eat out are lunch at 12 noon or 1pm and dinner at about 8pm.

Eating in

Fact file

Breakfast is coffee (or tea or hot chocolate) with a *croissant*, *pain grillé* (toast) or *tartine* (bread with butter and jam). At home *café au lait* (coffee and plenty of hot milk) served in a bowl is standard and it's fine to dunk whatever you are eating.

Meals are often three courses. Salad can be a separate course. Cheese comes before dessert which is often fruit.

Enjoy your meal.
Bon appétit!

I'm hungry/thirsty.
J'ai faim/soif.

I'm not hungry/thirsty.
Je n'ai pas faim/soif.

A table!
It's ready.

Servez-vous!
Help yourselves.

C'est fait avec quoi?
What's in this?

Tu peux me passer le beurre?
Can you pass the butter?

Ça me suffit, merci.
I've had enough thanks.

Tu veux de la salade?
Would you like some salad?

C'était délicieux.
That was delicious.

Un tout petit peu.
Just a little.

Encore un morceau de pain?
Some more bread?

Helping

> *Je peux vous aider?*
> **Can I help?**

> *Je peux mettre la table?*
> **May I set the table?**

> *Je peux faire la vaisselle?*
> **May I do the dishes?**

meal	le repas	**rice**	du riz
breakfast	le petit déjeuner	**potatoes**	des pommes de terre
lunch	le déjeuner	**onions**	des oignons
dinner	le dîner	**garlic**	de l'ail
bowl	un bol	**tomatoes**	des tomates
glass	un verre	**peppers**	des poivrons
plate	une assiette	**green beans**	des haricots verts
knife	un couteau	**peas**	des petits pois
fork	une fourchette	**zucchini**	des courgettes
spoon	une cuillère	**eggplant**	des aubergines
cereal	des céréales	**spinach**	des épinards
bread	du pain	**cabbage**	du chou
jam	de la confiture	**cauliflower**	du chou-fleur
margarine	de la margarine	**chicory**	des endives
chicken	du poulet	**(endives)**	
pork	du porc	**raw**	cru/crue
beef	du boeuf	**(too) hot, spicy**	(trop) épicé/épicée
veal	du veau	**salty**	salé/salée
liver	du foie	**sweet**	sucré/sucrée
pasta	des pâtes		

Special cases

> *Je n'aime pas le poisson.*
> **I don't like fish.**

> *Je suis végétarien.†*
> **I'm a vegetarian.**

> *Je suis allergique aux oeufs.*
> **I'm allergic to eggs.**

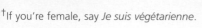

†If you're female, say *Je suis végétarienne.*

23

Shopping

Je peux vous aider?
Can I help you?

Je voudrais ça.
I'd like that.

Ça coûte combien?
How much is it?

Fact file

Opening times vary but keep in mind that many stores close for lunch and close on Monday. Most stores are open Tuesday to Saturday 9am to 12 noon and 2pm to 7pm. Small food stores may open on Sunday morning and others on Monday. Department stores and big supermarkets stay open all day Monday to Saturday. In the south, stores open earlier, close longer for lunch and stay open later. Look for signs on store doors: *Heures d'ouverture* (opening hours) or *Fermeture hebdomadaire* (closed each week on...)

A *tabac*, sometimes part of a bar, sells stamps, phonecards, candy etc., and may sell bus/*métro* tickets. *Drogueries* (hardware stores) sell handy things for camping but try a *magasin de sport* for actual camping equipment.

It is generally cheaper to buy everyday things in chain stores such as *Monoprix*, or in supermarkets such as *Casino*, rather than in smaller, specialist shops.

The cheapest, easiest way to buy food is in a super center or supermarket. Specialist food shops may be more pricey, but offer more choice and are worth a visit. *Charcuteries* or *traiteurs* (delicatessens) sell salads, quiches, pizzas, etc., as well as *charcuterie* (cured and cold meats, pâté, salami, etc.) In small places with no bakery, the sign *dépôt de pain* means fresh bread is stocked. Markets are held regularly and are good for food, local produce, cheap clothes, etc. People buy fruit and vegetables from market stalls, supermarkets or a *supérette* (small supermarket).

Vous pouvez me l'écrire s'il vous plaît?
Please write that down.

Très bien.
That's fine.

C'est quatorze euros.
It's 14 euros.

Je le prends.
I'll take it.

main shopping area	un centre commercial
store, shop	un magasin
department store	un grand magasin
market	un marché
super center, mega mart	un hypermarché
supermarket	un supermarché, un libre-service
small supermarket	une supérette
grocery store	une épicerie
bakery	une boulangerie
pastry shop	une pâtisserie
candy shop	une confiserie
butcher's shop	une boucherie
delicatessen	une charcuterie, un traiteur
fruit/vegetable stand	un marchand de fruits et légumes
fishmarket	une poissonnerie
healthfood shop	un magasin de produits diététiques
hardware store	une droguerie, une quincaillerie
pharmacy	une pharmacie
camera shop	un magasin de photos
gift shop	un magasin de cadeaux
tobacco shop	un tabac, un bar-tabac
newsstand	un marchand de journaux
bookstore	une librairie
stationery store	une papeterie
music store	un magasin de disques, un disquaire
computer store	un magasin d'informatique
flea market	un marché aux puces
junk shop	une brocante
sporting goods store	un magasin de sport
shoe store	un magasin de chaussures
shoe repairs	un talon minute
hair stylist, barber	un coiffeur
self-service laundry	une laverie automatique
travel agent	une agence de voyages
browsers welcome	entrée libre
open	ouvert/ouverte
closed	fermé/fermée
entrance	l'entrée
exit	la sortie
checkout, register	la caisse
stairs	l'escalier
price	le prix

Où sont les magasins?
Where's the main shopping area?

Vous vendez des piles?
Do you sell batteries?

Où est-ce que je peux en trouver?
Where can I get some?

Où est-ce que je peux faire réparer ça?
Where can I get this repaired?

Où est-ce que je peux trouver des lunettes de soleil?
Where's a good place for sunglasses?

Shopping

Je peux vous aider?
May I help you?

Je peux voir ça?
May I see that?

Il coûte combien?
How much is it?

Je regarde seulement.
I'm just looking.

Je vais réfléchir.
I'll think about it.

Je voudrais une crème solaire.
I need some suntan lotion.

Il n'y a pas plus grand?
Is there a bigger one?

sunscreen	un écran total
makeup	du maquillage
(hair) gel	du gel (pour les cheveux)
hair spray	de la laque
tampons	des tampons
tissues	des mouchoirs en papier
razor	un rasoir
shaving cream	de la crème à raser
painkiller	un calmant, un analgésique
contact lens solution	de la solution de nettoyage (pour des lentilles)
adhesive bandages	des pansements
film	une pellicule
English newspapers	des journaux anglais
postcard	une carte postale
writing paper	du papier à lettres
envelope	une enveloppe
notepad	un carnet
pen	un stylo
pencil	un crayon
poster	une affiche
stickers	des autocollants
badges	des badges
sunglasses	des lunettes de soleil
jewelry	des bijoux
watch	une montre
earrings	des boucles d'oreilles
ring	une bague
purse	un porte-monnaie
wallet	un portefeuille
bag	un sac
smaller	plus petit/petite
cheaper	moins cher/chère
another color	d'une autre couleur

Je voudrais une baguette.
I'd like a baguette.

Je voudrais pour quatre euros de raisin.
Can I have 4 euros worth of grapes?

Je voudrais une petite tranche de ce pâté.
Can I have a small piece of that pâté?

grocery bag	un sac plastique	chips	des chips
small	petit/petite	apples	des pommes
big	gros/grosse	pears	des poires
a slice of	une tranche de	peaches	des pêches
a little more	un peu plus	nectarines	des brugnons, des nectarines
a little less	un peu moins		
a serving of	une part de	plums	des prunes
a piece of	un morceau de	cherries	des cerises
a kilogram	un kilo	raspberries	des framboises
250 grams	deux cent cinquante grammes	strawberries	des fraises
		melon	un melon
organic	biologique, naturel	pineapple	un ananas
French salami	du saucisson		
quiche	une quiche		
bread	du pain		
roll	un petit pain		
cake	un gâteau		
croissant	un croissant		
donut	un beignet		
candy	des bonbons		
chocolate	du chocolat		

Fact file

For a change from *croissants*, try *un pain au chocolat/aux raisins* (pastry filled with chocolate/currants), or *une brioche* (a soft, slightly sweet loaf or bun). *Une ficelle* is a thin *baguette*. Wholegrain bread is *du pain complet*.

Un peu plus, s'il vous plaît.
A little more please.

Comme ça?
Like that?

Oui, ça suffit, merci.
OK, that's enough, thanks.

clothes	les vêtements
shirt	une chemise
T-shirt	un tee-shirt
tank top	un débardeur
sweatshirt	un sweat-shirt
sweater	un pull
fleece	une polaire
dress	une robe
skirt	une jupe
pants	un pantalon
shorts	un short
jogging bottoms	un pantalon de jogging
top	le haut
bottom	le bas
tennis shoes	des baskets
shoes	des chaussures
sandals	des sandales
boots	des bottes
belt	une ceinture
jacket	une veste
raincoat	un imper(méable)
underwear	un slip
panties	un slip, une culotte
bra	un soutien-gorge
pantyhose	un collant
socks	des chaussettes
swimsuit, trunks	un maillot (de bain)
a small size	une petite taille
a medium size	une taille moyenne

Fact file

You can usually exchange purchases within 28 days. For cheap clothes, try stores such as *Eurodif* or *Distri-Center*, or super centers. *Un dépôt-vente de vêtements* is a second-hand clothes store and *un magasin de dégriffés* is a designer seconds store. You will also come across charity stores.

a large size	une grande taille
too big	trop grand/grande
smaller	plus petit/petite
long	long/longue
short	court/courte
tight	serré/serrée
baggy	large
style	un style
look	un look
fashionable	à la mode
trendy, cool	branché/branchée*
untrendy	ringard/ringarde*
out-of-date	démodé/démodée
stylish	chic
dressy	habillé/habillée
scruffy	craignos*, minable
second-hand	d'occasion
fun	chouette*
sale	les soldes
dressing room	la cabine d'essayage

On peut venir en jean?
Are jeans all right?

Je peux emprunter ta veste?
Can I borrow your jacket?

J'apporte mon maillot?
Shall I bring my swimming stuff?

Music

Où est-ce que je peux acheter des CD†?
Where's a good place to buy CDs?

Can I put some music on?
Je peux mettre de la musique?
I listen to (lots of)...
J'écoute (beaucoup de)...
I've never heard any...
Je n'ai jamais entendu de...
Can you play this for me?
Vous vous pouvez me faire écouter ça?

Can you copy this for me?
Tu peux me copier ça?
Turn it up.
Plus fort.
It's too loud.
C'est trop fort.
Turn it down.
Baisse le volume.

Tu as vu le DVD?
Have you seen the DVD?

Vous avez ça en CD?
Do you have this on CD?

Vous avez un rayon jazz?
Do you have a jazz section?

C'est de qui?
Who's this by?

Playing an instrument

Do you play an instrument?
Tu joues d'un instrument?

Which instrument do you like best?
Quel instrument tu préfères?

I play the guitar.
Je joue de la guitare.

I play in a band.
Je joue dans un groupe.

I'm learning the drums.
J'apprends la batterie.

I sing in a band.
Je chante dans un groupe.

Quel genre de musique tu aimes?
What kind of music do you like?

Tu as écouté le dernier album?
Have you heard the latest album?

Ils sont nuls
They're useless.

Je peux emprunter l'album?
Can I borrow the album?

Il est génial.
It's great.

†Pronounced *say-day.*

music	la musique
music store	un magasin de disques, un disquaire
radio	la radio
(radio) station	une station
CD	un CD
CD player	un lecteur CD
stereo	une chaîne hi-fi
speakers	les baffles, les enceintes
headphones	des écouteurs
single	un single
album	un album
MP3 player	un MP3
downloadable music	de la musique à télécharger
a blank CD	un CD vierge
music/rock video	un clip
track	un morceau
song	une chanson
lyrics	les paroles
tune, melody	un air
rhythm, beat	le rythme
live	en direct
group, band	un groupe
orchestra	un orchestre
solo	en solo
singer	un chanteur/une chanteuse
accompaniment	l'accompagnement
fan	un fan
tour	une tournée
concert, gig	un concert
charts	le hit-parade
the Top 50	le Top 50 (cinquante)
number one	le numéro un
hit	un tube
latest	dernier/dernière
new	nouveau/nouvelle
piano	le piano
keyboards	le clavier
synthesizer	le synthétiseur
electric guitar	la guitare électrique
bass guitar	la guitare basse
acoustic guitar	la guitare acoustique
saxophone	le saxophone
trumpet	la trompette
accordion	l'accordéon
violin	le violon
flute	la flûte

Types of music

This list includes music you're likely to hear in France. For other types of music, try using the English word as the names are often the same.

house music	la house music
heavy metal	le heavy metal
rock	le rock
rap	le rap
hip-hop	le hip-hop
techno	la techno
reggae	le reggae
funk	la musique funk
soul	la musique soul
world music	les musiques du monde
rock & roll	le rock'n'roll
jazz	le jazz
blues	le blues
folk	le folk
pop	la musique pop
dance, disco	le disco
70's music	la musique des années 70 (soixante-dix)
retro	rétro
classical	la musique classique

Going out: making arrangements, sightseeing

> Alors, qu'est-ce qu'on fait?
> **What are we doing?**

> Tu as une idée?
> **Do you have any ideas?**

> On fait quelque chose ce soir?
> **Shall we do something tonight?**

> Non, je ne peux pas.
> **No, I can't.**

> A quelle heure?
> **What time?**

> Où est-ce qu'on se retrouve?
> **Where shall we meet?**

> On se voit devant la fontaine.
> **See you at the fountain.**

What is there to see here?	Qu'est-ce qu'il y a à voir ici?
Is there an admission charge?	Il faut payer l'entrée?
Is there a discount for students?	Il y a une réduction pour les étudiants?
Can I get a ticket in advance?	Je peux prendre un billet à l'avance?
Do you know a good place to...	Tu connais un endroit bien pour...
go dancing?	aller danser?
listen to music?	écouter de la musique?
eat?	aller manger?
go for a drink?	aller prendre un pot*?
I'm busy tonight.	Je suis pris/prise ce soir.
What time does it...	A quelle heure ça...
start?	commence?
finish?	finit?
open?	ouvre?
close?	ferme?
today	aujourd'hui
tomorrow	demain
day after tomorrow	après-demain
(in the) morning	le matin
(in the) afternoon	l'après-midi
(in the) evening	le soir
this week	cette semaine
next week	la semaine prochaine
no performance tonight	ce soir, relâche
entertainment guide, listing	un programme des spectacles
club, nightclub	une boîte (de nuit)
disco	une boîte, une discothèque
rave	une rave
party	une fête, une boum
picnic	un pique-nique
show, entertainment	un spectacle
(to the) movies	(au) cinéma
(to the) theater	(au) théâtre
ballet	un ballet
opera	un opéra
ticket office	le guichet
student ticket	un billet étudiant
performance, movie showing	une séance
guide book	un guide

Je ne veux rien faire.
I don't want to do anything.

Qu'est-ce que tu veux faire?
What do you want to do?

Si on allait en boîte?
Let's go to a club.

Qui est-ce qui joue au Jazz Bar?
Who's playing at the Jazz Bar?

Fact file

To find out what to visit, go to the tourist office (see page 6). You will get free information, leaflets and maps.

For what's on in Paris, look at *Pariscope* or *L'officiel des spectacles* (listings magazines), any daily newspaper, or local English magazines. Elsewhere, look at the local newspaper. Movies are often in version originale or *v.o.* (original language) with subtitles. *Version française* or *v.f.* (French version) means a movie has been dubbed into French. Student discounts are common.

Qu'est-ce qui passe?
What's on?

On passe un bon film quelque part?
Are there any good films on?

tour	une visite	**church**	une église
region	la région	**castle**	un château
countryside	la campagne	**tower**	une tour
mountains	la montagne	**city walls**	les remparts
lake	le lac	**ruins**	des ruines
river	la rivière	**caves**	des grottes
coast	la côte	**amusement arcade**	une salle de jeux
on the beach	à la plage	**theme park**	un parc d'attractions
in town	en ville	**festival**	une fête, un festival
at X's place	chez X	**fireworks**	un feu d'artifice
museum	un musée	**sound and light show**	un spectacle son et lumière
art gallery	un musée d'art		
exhibition	une exposition	**wine tasting**	une dégustation de vin
craft exhibition	une exposition artisanale	**interesting**	intéressant/intéressante
the old town	la vieille ville	**dull, boring**	ennuyeux/ennuyeuse
cathedral	la cathédrale	**beautiful**	beau/belle

movie theater	le cinéma	**author**	l'auteur
movie society/ club	un ciné-club, une cinémathèque	**director (movie)**	le réalisateur/la réalisatrice
		cast	les acteurs
theater	le théâtre	**actor/actress**	l'acteur/l'actrice
library	une bibliothèque	**movie buff**	un mordu/une mordue*
movie	un film		du cinéma
play	une pièce	**production**	une réalisation
book	un livre, un bouquin*	**plot**	l'intrigue
magazine	un magazine, une revue	**story**	l'histoire
comic	une BD, une bande dessinée	**set**	le décor
		special effects	les effets spéciaux
novel	un roman	**photography**	la photographie
poetry	la poésie	**TV**	la télé*

cable TV	la télé* câblée
satellite TV	la télé* par satellite
digital TV	la télé* numérique
program	le programme
channel	la chaîne
news	les informations, les actualités, le journal
weather	la météo
documentary	un documentaire
cartoons	des dessins animés
game show	un jeu télévisé
series	un feuilleton
soap	un mélo*
ads	la pub*
dubbed	doublé/doublée
in English	en anglais
with subtitles	sous-titré/titrée
well-known	très connu/connue
award-winning	primé/primée
avant-garde	d'avant-garde, expérimental
blockbuster	une superproduction
a classic	un classique
comedy	une comédie
thriller	un thriller
musical	une comédie musicale
horror movie	un film d'épouvante

adventure story	une histoire d'aventure
war movie	un film de guerre
detective movie	un film policier
sci-fi	la science-fiction
suspense	le suspense
sex	le sexe
violence	la violence
political	politique
satirical	satirique
serious	sérieux/sérieuse
offbeat	original/originale
commercial	commercial/commerciale
exciting, gripping	passionnant/passionnante
over the top	exagéré/exagérée
good	bon/bonne
OK, not bad	pas mauvais/pas mauvaise
bad, lousy	mauvais/mauvaise
silly	bête
funny	drôle, amusant, marrant/marrante*
sad	triste
It's scary.	Ça fait peur.
Where can I rent a DVD?	Où est-ce que je peux louer une DVD?
Do I have to be a member?	Je dois être adhérent/adhérente?

Je peux emprunter quelque chose à lire?
Can I borrow something to read?

J'ai étudié ce bouquin* à l'école.
I read that book at school.

Ça parle de quoi?
What's it about?

C'est génial.
It's great.

Tu as lu ça?
Have you read this?

C'est rasoir.*
It's so boring.

C'est de qui?
Who's it by?

Talking about yourself

Tu es toute seule?
Are you alone?

Tu as des soeurs?
Do you have any sisters?

Où est-ce que tu loges?
Where are you staying?

Non, je voyage avec des amis.
No, I'm traveling with friends.

I'm English.
Je suis anglais/anglaise.

My family is from...
Ma famille vient de...

I've been here for two weeks.
Je suis ici depuis deux semaines.

I'm on an exchange.
J'ai fait un échange.

I'm on vacation.
Je suis en vacances.

I'm staying with friends.
Je suis chez des amis.

I am a friend of...
Je suis un ami/une amie de...

I'm studying French.
J'étudie le français.

I'm traveling around.
Je voyage.

My parents are divorced.
Mes parents sont divorcés.

My birthday is on the...
Mon anniversaire est le...

I'm an only child.
Je suis fils/fille unique.

My name is...	Je m'appelle...
I live...	J'habite...
in the country	à la campagne
in a town	en ville
in the suburbs	en banlieue
by the sea	au bord de la mer
in a house	dans une maison
in an apartment	dans un appartement
I live with...	J'habite chez...
I don't live with...	Je n'habite pas chez...
my	mon (m), ma (f), mes (plural)
your	ton (m), ta (f), tes (plural)
family	la famille
parents	les parents
father/mother	le père/la mère
stepfather	le beau-père
stepmother	la belle-mère
husband/wife	le mari/la femme
boyfriend	le petit ami, le copain*
girlfriend	la petite amie, la copine*
brother/sister	le frère/la soeur
step/half brother	le demi-frère
step/half sister	la demi-soeur
alone	seul/seule
single	célibataire
married	marié/mariée
last name	le nom de famille
nickname	le surnom
my address	mon adresse
my e-mail address	mon adresse e-mail

Other people

Tu connais Alain?
Do you know Alain?

Il est grand.
He's tall.

Je ne peux pas la voir.
I can't stand her.

Qui est-ce?
Who's that?

Il est marrant.
He's a good laugh.

Il me plaît bien.
I like him.

Qu'est-ce qu'elle est devenue, Brigitte?
What's happened to Brigitte?

Elle est comment?
What's she like?

Elle est assez jolie.
She's fairly pretty.

On s'entend bien.
We get along OK.

friend	un ami/une amie, un copain/une copine	**tall**	grand/grande
boy	un garçon	**short**	petit/petite
girl	une fille	**fat**	gros/grosse
guy	un type, un mec*	**thin**	mince
someone	quelqu'un	**fair**	blond/blonde
has long hair	a les cheveux longs	**dark**	brun/brune
short hair	les cheveux courts	**pretty**	joli/jolie
curly hair	les cheveux frisés	**good-looking**	beau/belle
straight hair	les cheveux raides	**OK (looks)**	pas mal
has brown eyes	a les yeux marron	**not good-looking**	pas beau/pas belle
he/she is...	il/elle est...	**ugly**	laid/laide, moche*
		a little	un peu

Tu connais quelqu'un ici?
Do you know anyone here?

Tu veux boire quelque chose?
Do you want a drink?

C'est quoi, ton numéro de téléphone?
What's your phone number?

Tu veux danser?
Do you want to dance?

very	très, vachement*	**an idiot, a jerk**	un crétin/une crétine*
so	tellement	**in a bad mood**	de mauvaise humeur
really	vraiment	**in a good mood**	de bonne humeur
completely	complètement	**angry, annoyed**	fâché/fâchée
nice, OK	sympa*	**depressed**	déprimé/déprimée
not nice, horrible	pas sympa*	**happy**	heureux/heureuse
horrible, nasty	mauvais/mauvaise, vache**		
cool, trendy, hip	branché/branchée*		
old-fashioned	ringard/ringarde*	**Have you heard that... ?**
clever	doué/douée	Tu sais que... ?
thick	bête	
boring	rasoir*	**Brigitte is going out with Alain.**
shy	timide	Brigitte sort avec Alain.
nuts, crazy	fou/folle, dingue*	
weird	bizarre	**Luc went with Sylvie.**
lazy	paresseux/paresseuse	Luc a une touche avec Sylvie.
laid back	relax*, relaxe*	
up-tight	coincé/coincée	**He/She kissed me.**
mixed up, untogether	compliqué/compliquée	Il/Elle m'a embrassé/embrassée.
selfish	égoïste	**They split up.**
jealous	jaloux/jalouse	Ils ont rompu/cassé*.
rude	grossier/grossière	
macho	macho	**We had a fight.**
stuck up	snob	On s'est disputé.
loaded, rich	friqué/friquée*	
cool	cool*	**Leave me alone.**
a creep	un minable, un pauvre type	Laissez-moi tranquille.
		Laisse-moi tranquille.

On peut se revoir?
Can I see you again?

Je peux venir aussi?
Can I come too?

Désolé, je ne peux pas.
Sorry I can't.

Tu veux venir?
Want to come?

Peut-être une autre fois.
Maybe some other time.

Sports

Tu fais du sport?
Do you play any sports?

Tu fais du jogging?
Do you go jogging?

Je ne suis vraiment pas en forme.
I'm really unfit.

Je joue au rugby.
I play rugby.

Je ne joue pas au squash.
I don't play squash.

Tu joues au tennis?
Do you play tennis?

Tous les combien?
How often?

Tu veux faire une partie de badminton?
Do you want to play a game of badminton?

Je n'ai pas de raquette.
I don't have a racket.

Je fais du jogging tous les matins.
I go jogging every morning.

Catch!
Attrape!

In!/Out!
In!/Out!

Throw it to me.
Lance-le moi.

Who won?
Qui a gagné?

You're cheating!
Tu triches!

How do you play this?
Comment on joue à ça?

What are the rules?
Quelles sont les règles?

What team do you support?
Tu es pour quelle équipe?

Is there a match we could go to?
Il y a un match qu'on pourrait aller voir?

Fact file

Soccer, tennis, basketball and volleyball are popular games. Rugby is played a lot in the south and south west. Cycling is very popular, and the biggest spectator event is the annual *Tour de France*, a three week cycle race. In the south particularly, people of all ages play *boules* or *pétanque* (both played with metal balls, often on a patch of ground in the town square). Winter sports are very popular, with downhill skiing in the Alps and Pyrenees, but also cross-country in the Jura, Vosges and Massif Central.

sports	un sport	sports uniform	les vêtements de sport
match	un match		
a game (of)	une partie (de)	once a week	une fois par semaine
doubles	double	twice a week	deux fois par semaine
singles	simple		
race	une course	I play...	Je joue au...
marathon	un marathon	I don't play...	Je ne joue pas au...
championships	les championnats	tennis	tennis
Olympics	les Jeux Olympiques	squash	squash
World Cup	la Coupe du Monde	badminton	badminton
club	un club	soccer	foot(ball)
team	une équipe	football	football américain
referee	un arbitre	basketball	basket
supporter	un supporter	volleyball	volley
training, practice	l'entraînement	table tennis	ping-pong
a goal	un but	baseball	base-ball
to lose	perdre	I do, I go...	Je fais...
a draw	match nul	judo	du judo
sports center	le centre sportif	karate	du karaté
stadium	le stade	jogging	du jogging
gym	le gymnase	running	de la course à pied
court	le court	aerobics	de l'aérobic
indoor	couvert/couverte	weight-training	des poids et haltères
outdoor	en plein air	body-building	de la musculation
ball (small)	la balle	keep-fit, gym	de la gym
ball (large)	le ballon	bowling	du bowling
net	le filet	dancing	de la danse
athletic shoes	des chaussures de sport	yoga	du yoga
tennis shoes	des tennis	I don't do, go...	Je ne fais pas de[†]...

Quel est le score?
What's the score?

Tape!
Kick it!

Ici!
Here!

Vite!
Quick!

Je peux jouer?
Can I play?

Passe le ballon.
Pass the ball.

Cours!
Run!

[†]When saying *Je ne fais pas*, don't use *du, de la, de l'* or *des*. Use *de* instead, ex. *Je ne fais pas de judo.*   **41**

Je n'aime pas trop la plongée sous-marine.
I'm not big on scuba diving.

J'adore le deltaplane.
I love hang gliding.

Je préfère le ski nautique.
I prefer water-skiing.

Je n'ai jamais essayé.
I've never tried.

Je ne sais pas nager.
I can't swim.

Les courants sont forts?
Are the currents strong?

Ce n'est pas dangereux?
It's not dangerous, is it?

I like...	J'aime...
I don't like...	Je n'aime pas...
I love ...	J'adore...
I prefer...	Je préfère...
swimming	la natation
(scuba) diving	la plongée (sous-marine)
sailing	faire de la voile
surfing	le surf
canoeing	faire du canoë
rowing	faire de l'aviron
sunbathing	me faire bronzer
boat	un bateau
sail	la voile
surfboard	une planche de surf
windsurfer	une planche à voile
sea	la mer
beach	la plage
swimming pool	la piscine
in the sun	au soleil
in the shade	à l'ombre
mask	un masque
snorkel	un tuba
flippers	des palmes
wetsuit	une combinaison de plongée
life jacket	un gilet de sauvetage
fishing	la pêche
fishing rod	la canne à pêche

Tu as déjà fait de l'escalade?
Have you ever been climbing?

Je peux prendre des leçons?
Can I get lessons?

C'est cher?
Is it expensive?

Où est-ce que je peux louer des skis?
Where can I rent skis?

Tu aimes faire du patin à glace?
Do you like skating?

cycling	le cyclisme
racing bike	un vélo de course
mountain bike	un vélo tout terrain, un VTT
touring bike	un vélo de randonnée
BMX	un BMX
horse riding	l'équitation
horse	un cheval
walking, hiking	la marche à pied
footpath	un chemin (de randonnée)
skateboarding	faire du skateboard
roller skating	faire des rollers
ice rink	une patinoire
skates	des patins
skiing	faire du ski
cross-country skiing	le ski de fond
snowboarding	le surf des neiges
ski run	une piste de ski
ski pass	un forfait
ski lifts	les remontées mécaniques
chair lift	le télésiège
drag lift	le téléski, le tire-fesses*
skis	des skis
ski boots	des chaussures de ski
ski goggles	des lunettes de ski
snow	la neige

Je suis un débutant.
I'm a beginner.

Je suis assez bon.
I'm pretty good.

J'en ai assez.
I've had enough.

Allez, tu vas y arriver.
Come on, you can do it.

43

Studying

Qu'est-ce que tu fais?
What do you do?

Où est-ce que tu fais tes études?
Where are you studying?

C'est quel genre de lycée?
What sort of college is it?

A quelle heure tu sors?
What time do you finish?

Tu as beaucoup de travail?
Do you have a lot of work?

Oui, plein.
Yes, loads.

I do...	Je fais...
computer studies	de l'informatique
math	des maths
physics	de la physique
chemistry	de la chimie
biology	de la biologie
natural sciences	des sciences naturelles, des sciences nat
geography	de la géographie
history	de l'histoire
economics	de l'économie
business studies	des études commerciales
languages	des langues
French	du français
English	de l'anglais
Spanish	de l'espagnol
German	de l'allemand
literature	de la littérature
philosophy	de la philosophie, de la philo
sociology	de la sociologie, de la socio
psychology	de la psychologie, de la psycho
religious studies	de l'instruction religieuse
general studies	de l'éducation civique
design and technology	du dessin industriel et de la techno
art	du dessin, des arts plastiques
drama	du théâtre
music	de la musique
PE	de la gym
school	une école, un bahut*
mixed	mixte
boarding school	un internat
private school	un collège privé
term	un trimestre
vacation	les vacances
beginning of term	la rentrée

school club	un club, un foyer
class representative	le délégué/la déléguée de classe
lesson, lecture	un cours
tuition, coaching, private lessons	des cours particuliers, du soutien
homework	des devoirs
essay	une dissertation
translation	une traduction
project	un projet
coursework, presentation	un exposé
review, study	la révision
test	un contrôle
oral	oral/orale
written	écrit/écrite
continuous assessment	le contrôle continu
grade	la note
teacher, lecturer	le professeur, le/la prof
(language) assistant	l'assistant/l'assistante
good	bon/bonne
bad	mauvais/mauvaise
strict	strict/stricte, sévère
easy going	pas strict/stricte, sympa
discipline	la discipline
to repeat (a year)	redoubler
suspended	renvoyé/renvoyée temporairement
expelled	renvoyé/renvoyée
to skip a lesson	sauter un cours
a grant	une bourse

I'm a student.
Je suis étudiant/ étudiante.

I'm still at school.
Je vais encore à l'école.

I want to do...
J'aimerais faire...

He is goofing off.
Il fait l'école buissonnière.

Fact file

Types of schools and colleges include *un collège* (comprehensive-type school for the first four years of high school), *un lycée d'enseignement professionnel* (high school with vocational bias), *un lycée* (similar to an elementary school), *un IUT* or *institut universitaire de technologie* (polytechnic), *une université* or *une faculté*, often shortened to *fac* (university), and *une haute école* (élite university with entry by *concours* (competitive exam)). Most schools are mixed and students don't wear uniforms. Summer vacation runs from late June to early September. Schools employ *surveillants* or *pions** to keep discipline.

Junior high starts at about age 11 with *sixième* form and goes up to *première* and finally *terminale*. At about 16, most pupils get the *brevet* certificate, based on average grades. Many pupils go on to take the *CAP* or *BEP* (vocational exams), the *HT* (more technological), or *bac* – short for *baccalauréat* – which gives access to universities. School is mandatory until age 16.

Tu veux faire quoi après le lycée?
What do you want to do when you finish college?

Tu étudies quelles matières?
What subjects are you doing?

Quand est-ce que tu passes tes examens?
When are your exams?

Tu es en quelle classe?
What year are you in?

Qu'est-ce que tu préfères?
What do you like best?

45

Je travaille dans un magasin.
I work in a store.

C'est quoi, tes loisirs?
What kind of things do you do in your spare time?

Tu as beaucoup de temps libre?
Do you have a lot of spare time?

J'aime bien la photographie.
I'm interested in photography.

J'ai un PC.
I've got a PC.

Etes-vous sur Internet?
Are you on the internet?

Sur quelles touches je dois appuyer?
What keys do I have to press?

Qu'est-ce que je fais maintenant?
What do I do now?

C'est à qui?
Whose turn is it?

I do a lot of sports.	Je fais beaucoup de sport.
I listen to a lot of music.	J'écoute beaucoup de musique.
I write songs.	J'écris des chansons.
I like gaming.	J'aime les jeux vidéos.
I work in a café.	Je travaille dans un café.
I babysit.	Je fais du baby-sitting.

I collect...	Je fais collection de...
seashells	coquillages
all kinds of things	plein de trucs*
I like...	J'aime...
drawing	le dessin
painting	la peinture
acting	faire du théâtre
making jewelry	faire des bijoux
a part-time job	un petit boulot
allowance	de l'argent de poche
computer	un ordinateur
laptop	un (ordinateur) portable
software	un logiciel
computer games	des jeux électroniques
word processing	le traitement de texte
website	un site Web
disk	un disque
joystick	la manette de jeu
mouse	la souris
game	un jeu
chess	les échecs
board games	les jeux de société
cards	les cartes
foosball	le baby-foot
What are the rules?	Quelles sont les règles?
My turn.	C'est à moi.
Your turn.	C'est a toi.

46

What do you want to do later?	**I want...**	Je voudrais...
Tu veux faire quoi, plus tard?	**to live/work overseas**	habiter/travailler à l'étrange.
When I finish...	**to travel**	voyager
Quand j'aurai fini...	**to have a career**	faire une carrière
One day...	**to get a good job**	trouver un bon boulot
Un jour...	**to get my**	obtenir mes diplômes
I want to be a...	**qualifications**	
Je voudrais être...	**to keep studying**	poursuivre mes études

What do you think about...?	**I think...**	**You're right.**
Qu'est-ce que tu penses de...?	Je pense...	Tu as raison.
I don't know much about...	**I belong to...**	**I don't agree.**
Je ne sais pas grand-chose sur...	J'appartiens à...	Je ne suis pas d'accord.
Can you explain...?	**I believe in...**	**I'm for, I support...**
Tu peux/Vous pouvez expliquer...?	Je crois à...	Je suis pour...
I feel angry about (pollution).	**I don't believe in...**	**I'm against...**
(La pollution), ça me met en colère.	Je ne crois pas à...	Je suis contre...

the future	l'avenir	**greenhouse effect**	l'effet de serre
(in) the past	(dans) le passé	**ozone layer**	la couche d'ozone
now, nowadays	de nos jours, maintenant	**deforestation**	le déboisement
religion	la religion	**nuclear power**	l'énergie nucléaire
god	dieu	**recycling**	le recyclage
human rights	les droits de l'homme	**politics**	la politique
gay	gay, homo	**government**	le gouvernement
feminist	féministe	**democratic**	démocratique
abortion	l'avortement	**elections**	des élections
drugs	les drogues	**party**	un parti
drug addict	un drogué/une droguée	**revolution**	une révolution
HIV positive	séropositif/séropositive	**the left**	la gauche
Aids	le Sida	**the right**	la droite
unemployment	le chômage	**fascist**	fasciste
Third World	le Tiers-Monde	**communist**	communiste
peace	la paix	**socialist**	socialiste
war	la guerre	**environmentalists**	les écologistes
terrorism	le terrorisme	**conservative**	conservateur/
environment	l'environnement		conservatrice
pollution	la pollution	**reactionary**	réactionnaire, réac*
nature conservation	la sauvegarde	**politically**	engagé/engagée
	de la nature	**active**	
global warming	le réchauffement de la	**march, demo**	une manifestation,
	planète		une manif*

problems, emergencies

am sick.	Je suis malade.
t hurts.	Ça fait mal.
It hurts a lot.	Ça fait très mal.
It hurts a little.	Ça fait un peu mal.
It itches.	Ça me démange.
I've cut myself.	Je me suis coupé/coupée.
I think I've broken my...	Je crois que je me suis cassé...
I've been stung by a wasp.	J'ai été piqué/piquée par une guêpe.
I've got mosquito bites.	J'ai été piqué/piquée par des moustiques.
He/She's had too much to drink.	Il/Elle a trop bu.
I feel dizzy.	J'ai la tête qui tourne.
I'm constipated.	Je suis constipé/constipée.
I'm on medication for...	Je prends des médicaments pour...
I'm allergic...	Je suis allergique...
to antibiotics	aux antibiotiques
to some medicines	à certains médicaments
I have...	J'ai...
food poisoning	un empoisonnement alimentaire
diarrhea	la diarrhée
heatstroke	un coup de soleil
a headache	mal à la tête
a stomachache	mal au ventre
my period	mes règles
an infection	une infection
a sore throat	mal à la gorge
a cold	un rhume
flu	la grippe
a cough	une toux
hayfever	le rhume des foins
asthma	de l'asthme
a toothache	mal aux dents
a temperature	de la température
the shivers	des frissons
a hangover	la gueule de bois*
doctor	le médecin, le docteur
female doctor	une femme médecin
dentist	le/la dentiste
optician	l'opticien/l'opticienne
pharmacy	la pharmacie
pill	un cachet, une pilule
injection	une piqûre

Je ne me sens pas bien.
I don't feel well.

Qu'est-ce qui ne va pas?
What's wrong?

Je vais vomir.
I'm going to be sick.

Je suis vraiment désolé.
I'm really sorry about this.

Il faut que je voie un médecin.
I need to see a doctor.

Il y a une pharmacie ouverte près d'ici?
Is there a pharmacy open around here?

Vous pouvez me donner quelque chose pour le rhume des foins?
Can you give me something for hayfever?

J'ai perdu une lentille.
I've lost my contact lens.

On m'a volé mes affaires.
Someone's stolen my things.

J'ai cassé mes lunettes.
I've broken my glasses.

Je n'ai pas vu ce qui s'est passé.
I didn't see what happened.

Fact file

In France everyone has to carry their identity card, so keep your passport with you. Don't be surprised if you are asked to show your *papiers* (documents, ID).

If you have to see a doctor or go to the *service des urgences* (casualty department) of the local *hôpital* (hospital), expect to pay, though not upfront in an emergency. You should be able to claim back expenses on insurance, but hang on to all the paperwork.

Emergencies

Emergency phone numbers: police 17; fire 18; ambulance 15. For very serious problems, contact the closest *Consultat Américain* (American Consulate).

There's been an accident.	Il vient d'y avoir un accident.
Help!	Au secours!
Fire!	Au feu!
Stop thief!	Au voleur!
Please call...	S'il vous plaît, appelez...
an ambulance	une ambulance
the police	la police
the fire department	les pompiers
the lifeguard	le maître-nageur

wallet	mon portefeuille
(hand)bag	mon sac (à main)
my things	mes affaires
my papers	mes papiers
my passport	mon passeport
my key	ma clé
my cell phone	mon portable
all my money	tout mon argent
lost property	objets perdus
I'm lost.	Je suis perdu/perdue.
I'm scared.	J'ai peur.
I'm in trouble.	J'ai des ennuis.

I need to talk to someone.
Il faut que je parle à quelqu'un.

I don't know what to do.
Je ne sais pas quoi faire.

I don't want to cause trouble, but...
Je ne veux pas faire d'ennuis, mais...

A man's following me.
Il y a un homme qui me suit.

Can you keep an eye on my things?
Vous pouvez surveiller mes affaires?

Has anyone seen...?
Quelqu'un a vu...?

Please don't smoke.
Ça vous ennuierait de ne pas fumer?

It doesn't work.
Ça ne marche pas.

There's no water/power.
Il n'y a pas d'eau/de courant.

This book has included informal French and slang where appropriate, but these two pages list a few of the most common words and phrases. When using slang it is easy to sound off-hand or rude without meaning to. Here, as in the rest of the book, a single asterisk after a word shows it is mild slang, but two asterisks show it can be rude and it may be safest to avoid using it. You will find more slang in the dictionary.

Alternative pronunciations

I don't know	j'sais pas* (je ne sais pas)
I haven't	j'ai pas* (je n'ai pas)
you have	t'as* (tu as)
you are	t'es* (tu es)
there is/are	y a*(il ay a)
yes	ouais* (oui)
well	ben* (bien)
nice, friendly	sympa (sympathique)

Abbreviations

crazy, keen	fana (fanatique)
ecologist	un écolo (écologiste)
intellectual	un intello (intellectuel)
teacher	un prof (professeur)
in the morning	du mat (du matin)
movie theater	le ciné (cinéma)
test	une interro (interrogation)
apartment	un appart (appartement)

Fillers and exclamations

OK	OK, bien, d'acc
right	bon, alors
well	eh bien
actually, in fact	en fait
by the way	au fait

American and English imports

le boss; cool; flipper **(to flip)**; un job; le look; non-stop; un scoop; sexy; le show-biz; un spot **(a commercial, an ad)**; le stress

very	hyper, super, vachemen
great, cool	génial/géniale, chouette, super*, terrible, d'enfer
trash, bad, disgusting	moche*, infect/infecte, nul, dégueulasse**
boring	chiant/chiante**
irritating, annoying	énervant/énervante
funny	marrant/marrante*
crazy, nuts	dingue*, cinglé/cinglée*
lucky	verni/vernie*
broke	fauché/fauchée, à sec*
guy	un type*, un mec*, un gars*
friend, buddy	un pote*
kid	un/une gosse*, un/une môme*
policeman	un flic*
money, cash	les sous, le fric*, le blé*, les ronds*, l'oseille
clothes	les fringues*
car	la bagnole*, la tire*, la caisse*
food, grub	la bouffe**
school	le bahut*
school, company	la boîte*
room	la piaule*
problem	un pépin*, un 'blem*
to have fun	se marrer*
to understand, get it	piger*, capter*
to talk trash	baratiner*
to chat up	baratiner*, draguer** brancher**
to steal	piquer*, faucher
to throw out, fire	virer
to crack up, lose it	craquer*
to fail, fall through	foirer*
to be careful	faire gaffe*
to be on good behavior	avoir une pêche d'enfer*
to be full of energy	avoir la frite*, avoir la pêche*
to work	bosser*
It's fabulous, great.	C'est le pied.*
You're getting on my nerves.	Tu m'énerves. Tu me gonfles.**
Leave me alone.	Fous-moi la paix.** Lâche-moi les baskets.**
I don't care.	Je m'en fous.*

Countries

country	le pays	**continent**	le continent
north	le nord	**south**	le sud
east	l'est	**west**	l'ouest

Africa	l'Afrique (f)
Algeria	l'Algérie (f)
Asia	l'Asie (f)
Australia	l'Australie (f)
Austria	l'Autriche (f)
Bangladesh	le Bangladesh
Belgium	la Belgique
Canada	le Canada
Caribbean Islands	les Petites Antilles (f)
Central America	l'Amérique Centrale (f)
China	la Chine
Corsica	la Corse
England	l'Angleterre (f)
Europe	l'Europe (f)
France	la France
Germany	l'Allemagne (f)
Great Britain	la Grande-Bretagne
Greece	la Grèce
Hungary	la Hongrie
India	l'Inde (f)
Ireland	l'Irlande (f)
Israel	Israël (m)
Italy	l'Italie (f)
Jamaica	la Jamaïque
Japan	le Japon
Martinique	la Martinique
Middle East	le Moyen-Orient
Morocco	le Maroc
Netherlands	les Pays-Bas
New Zealand	la Nouvelle-Zélande
North Africa	l'Afrique du Nord
Pakistan	le Pakistan
Poland	la Pologne
Russia	la Russie
Scotland	l'Écosse (f)
South America	l'Amérique du Sud (f)
Spain	l'Espagne (f)
Switzerland	la Suisse
Tunisia	la Tunisie
Turkey	la Turquie
United States	les Etats-Unis
Vietnam	le Viêt-Nam
Wales	le pays de Galles

Nationalities

You can say "I come from" + country:

Je viens du + (m) name ex. *Je viens du Japon*
Je viens de la + (f) name ex. *Je viens de la Suisse*
Je viens d' + names that start with a vowel ex. *Je viens d'Angleterre*
Je viens des + plural names ex. *Je viens des Etats-Unis.*

Or you can say "I am..." + adjective for nationality, ex. *Je suis*:

Algerian	algérien/algérienne
American	américain/américaine
Australian	australien/australienne
Austrian	autrichien/autrichienne
Belgian	belge
Canadian	canadien/canadienne
Dutch	hollandais/hollandaise
English	anglais/anglaise
French	français/française
German	allemand/allemande
Indian	indien/indienne
Irish	irlandais/irlandaise
Italian	italien/italienne
Moroccan	marocain/marocaine
Pakistani	pakistanais/pakistanaise
Scottish	écossais/écossaise
Spanish	espagnol/espagnole
Swiss	suisse
Welsh	gallois/galloise

Faiths

agnostic	un/une agnostique
atheist	un/une athée
Buddhist	bouddhiste
Catholic	catholique
Christian	chrétien/chrétienne
Hindu	hindou/hindoue
Jewish	juif/juive
Muslim	musulman/musulmane
Protestant	protestant/protestante
Sikh	sikh

Numbers

0 zéro	**31** trente et un
1 un	**40** quarante
2 deux	**50** cinquante
3 trois	**60** soixante
4 quatre	**70** soixante-dix
5 cinq	**71** soixante et onze
6 six	**72** soixante-douze
7 sept	**80** quatre-vingts
8 huit	**81** quatre-vingt-un
9 neuf	**82** quatre-vingt-deux
10 dix	**90** quatre-vingt-dix
11 onze	**91** quatre-vingt-onze
12 douze	**92** quatre-vingt-douze
13 treize	**100** cent
14 quatorze	**101** cent un
15 quinze	**200** deux cents
16 seize	**300** trois cents
17 dix-sept	**1,000** mille
18 dix-huit	**1,100** mille cent
19 dix-neuf	**1,200** mille deux cents
20 vingt	**2,000** deux mille
21 vingt et un	**2,100** deux mille cent
22 vingt-deux	**10,000** dix mille
23 vingt-trois	**100,000** cent mille
30 trente	**1,000,000** un million

Colors

light	clair/claire
dark	foncé/foncée
blue	bleu/bleue
navy	bleu marine
green	vert/verte
yellow	jaune
orange	orange
purple	mauve, violet/violette
pink	rose
red	rouge
white	blanc/blanche
grey	gris/grise
brown	brun/brune
black	noir/noire

Days and dates

Monday	lundi
Tuesday	mardi
Wednesday	mercredi
Thursday	jeudi
Friday	vendredi
Saturday	samedi
Sunday	dimanche
January	janvier
February	février
March	mars
April	avril
May	mai
June	juin
July	juillet
August	août
September	septembre
October	octobre
November	novembre
December	décembre
day	le jour
week	la semaine
month	le mois
year	l'année, l'an
diary	un agenda
calendar	un calendrier
yesterday	hier
the day before yesterday	avant-hier
today	aujourd'hui
the next day	le lendemain
tomorrow	demain
the day after tomorrow	après-demain
last week	la semaine dernière
this week	cette semaine
next week	la semaine prochaine
What's the date?	Quelle est la date?
on Mondays	le lundi
in August	en août
(on) 1st of April	le premier avril
(on) 2nd of January	le deux janvier
in the year 2000	en l'an deux mille
in 2012	en deux mille douze

Time

hour	l'heure
What time is it?	Quelle heure est-il?
It's 1 o'clock.	Il est une heure.
2 o'clock	deux heures
minute	la minute
morning	le matin
afternoon	l'après-midi
evening	le soir
noon	midi
midnight	minuit
quarter past two	deux heures et quart
half past two	deux heures et demie
quarter to two	deux heures moins le quart
five past two	deux heures cinq
ten to two	deux heures moins dix
What time... ?	A quelle heure... ?
in ten minutes	dans dix minutes
half an hour ago	il y a une demi-heure
at 09:00	à neuf heures
at 13:17	à treize heures dix-sept
at 9am	à neuf heures du matin
at 3pm	à trois heures de l'après-midi
at 9 in the evening	à neuf heures du soir

Seasons and weather

season	la saison	**sky**	le ciel
spring	le printemps	**sun**	le soleil
summer	l'été	**clouds**	les nuages
fall	l'automne	**rain**	la pluie
winter	l'hiver	**snow**	la neige

It's nice.	Il fait beau.
It's sunny.	Il fait soleil.
It's hot.	Il fait chaud.
It's windy.	Il fait du vent.
It's raining.	Il pleut.
It's foggy.	Il y a du brouillard.
It's snowing.	Il neige.
It's icy.	Il y a du verglas.
It's cold.	Il fait froid.
It's freezing.	Il gèle.
It's horrible.	Il fait mauvais.
What's the weather like?	
Quel temps fait-il?	

The fact files below focus on essential, practical information which is different from that given for France.

Fact file: Belgium

Languages – French is mostly spoken in the south, Flemish in the north. **Travel** – For under 26s, cheap deals include the *Go Pass* and the *Tourrail* card, both valid on the *SNCB* (Belgian railways). Taxis take up to four passengers but can be expensive. Mopeds can be ridden from age 16. **Banks and phones** – Currency is the euro. Banking hours are usually 9am-4pm with an hour's closure for lunch. In cities, some banks are open at lunchtime and on Saturday morning. Phones are card operated. **Shopping** – Opening times are 9am-6pm, or later on Friday. Stores close on Sunday and one other day. **Emergency phone numbers** – Police 101, fire and ambulance 100.

Fact file: Switzerland

Languages – The three official languages are French, German and Italian. **Travel** – Cheap deals include the *Swiss Pass, Swiss Flexi Pass* and *Half Fare Travel Card*, valid on trains, and most bus and lake steamer services. There are also various regional travel passes. To rent bikes from stations you must book the day before. You have to be 18 to ride a moped. **Banks and phones** – Currency is the Swiss *franc* (CHF). In cities banks open 8:30am-4:30pm on weekdays; elsewhere they close for lunch from 12 noon-2pm. Train stations and chain stores often change money. Phone booths mainly take *taxcards* (phonecards). **Shopping** – Opening times vary a lot. Some stores are closed on Monday mornings. **Emergencies** – There is no national health service so make sure you are insured. Phone numbers – police 117; fire 118; ambulance 144.

To pronounce French well, you need the help of a French speaker or some language CDs, but these general points will help you to make yourself understood. Bear in mind that there are exceptions and regional variations.

Vowel sounds

a sounds like "a" in cat.

e, *eu* and *oe* sound a little like "u" in "fur." At the end of a word, *e* is silent.

é sounds like "a" in "late", but a little clipped.

è, *ê* and *ai* sound like "ai" in "air."

i sounds like "i" in machine but clipped.

o sounds like "o" in soft.

ô, *au*, and *eau* sound like "o" in "bone."

u is a sharp "u" sound. Round your lips to say "oo", then try to say "ee", and you will be close.

oi sounds like "wa" in "wagon."

ou sounds like "oo" in "moody."

ui sounds like "wee" in "week."

Nasal sounds

French has some slightly nasal sounds in which the *n* or *m* are barely sounded:

an and *en* are a little like "aun" in "aunt."

am and *em* (when they precede *p* or *b*) sound like *an*/*en* but with a hint of an "m."

in (when it precedes a consonant or is at the end of a word) and *ain* sound a little like "an" in "can."

im (when it precedes *p* or *b*) sounds like *in*/*ain* but with a hint of an "m."

on is a bit like "on" in "song."

un (at the end of a word or before a consonant) is a bit like "an" in "an apple."

Consonants

c is hard as in "cat", except before *i* or *e*, or with a cedilla: *ç*. Then it is like "s" in "sun."

ch sounds like "sh" in "shoe."

g is like "g" in "go" except before *e* or *i*. Then it is soft like the "j" sound in "measure."

gn is like the "nio" sound in "onion."

h is never pronounced.

j is like the "j" sound in "measure."

ll when it follows *i* is like "y" in "young."

ail on the end of a word is like "y" in "sky."

qu is the same as a hard *c* (the "u" is silent).

r is made in the back of the throat.

s is like "z" in "zoo", and *ss* or *s* at the start of a word is like "s" in "soap."

Consonants at ends of words are usually silent unless an *e* comes after. At ends of words *er*, *et* and *ez* usually sound like *é*.

French alphabet

Applying the points above, this is how you say the alphabet: A, Bé, Çé, Dé, Eu, èFe, G = jé, acHe, I, Ji, Ka, èLe, èMe, èNe, O, Pé, Quu, èRe, èSse, Té, U, Vé, W = double-vé, iXe, Y = i-grèque, Zède.

Nouns

All French nouns are either masculine (m) or feminine (f).

For a few nouns the gender is obvious, ex. *le garçon* (boy) is masculine and *la fille* (girl) is feminine. For most nouns the gender seems random, ex. *le tronc* (trunk) is masculine and *la branche* (branch) is feminine. Some nouns can be either gender, ex. *le/la touriste* (tourist m/f) and some have two forms, ex. *l'étudiant/ l'étudiante* (student m/f).

The article (the word for "the" or "a") shows the gender of the noun: with masculine nouns "the" is *le*, ex. *le train* (the train) and "a" is *un*, ex. *un train* (a train); with feminine nouns, "the" is *la*, ex. *la boîte* (the box) and "a" is *une*, ex. *une boîte* (a box). With nouns that begin with a vowel and some nouns beginning with h, "the" is *l'*, ex. *l'avion* (the plane) or *l'heure* (the hour), but "a" is still *un* or *une*, ex. *un avion* (a plane) or *une heure* (an hour).

Sometimes French uses an article where English doesn't, ex. *J'aime le thé* (I like tea).

To help you get articles right, this book gives nouns with the article most likely to be useful, and the word list at the end of the book makes genders clear by listing nouns with *le* or *la*, or adding (m) or (f) after those that begin with a vowel.

Don't worry if you mix up *le* and *la*; you will still be understood. It is worth knowing the gender of nouns, though, since other words, especially adjectives, change to match them. Always learn a noun with *le* or *la* – or *un* or *une* for nouns beginning with a vowel. Many nouns ending in *e* are feminine.

Plurals

In the plural, the French for "the" is *les*, ex. *les trains* (the trains).

In English "some" (the plural for "a") is often left out. In French *un* or *une* becomes *des* in the plural and is always used, ex. *Il y a des types qui...* (There are guys who...)

To make a noun plural, add *s*, ex. *deux trains* (two trains). For some nouns you add *x*, ex. *deux gâteaux* (two cakes).

De, du, de la, de l', des (any, some)

When talking about things like butter or water, English uses "any," "some" or no article, ex. Is there any butter left? I want some butter. There's water in the pitcher.

French has a special article that is always used in these cases, *de* + "the;" but *de* + *le* become *du*, and *de* + *les* become *des*, so: *du* + (m) noun, ex. *Tu veux du café?* (Would you like some coffee?); *de la* + (f) noun, ex. *Tu as de la musique rock?* (Do you have any rock music?); *de l'* + nouns beginning with a vowel, ex. *Tu veux de l'eau gazeuse?* (Do you want any carbonated water?); *des* + plural nouns, ex. *Tu veux des frites?* (Do you want some french fries?) In negative sentences simply use *de* + noun, or *d'* before a vowel, ex. *Je ne veux pas de café/d'eau* (I don't want any coffee/ water).

De (of)

In French "of" is *de*. It works in the same way as *de* meaning "any, some:" with (m) nouns use *du*, ex. *la couleur du mur* (the color of the wall), and so on.

French uses "of" to show possession where English doesn't, ex. *le pull de Paul* (Paul's sweater, literally "the sweater of Paul.")

Au, à la, à l', aux (to, at)

The French for "to" and "at" is *à*. With *le* and *les*, *à* becomes *au* and *aux*, so use:
au + (m) nouns, ex. *Je vais au ciné* (I'm going to the movies);
à la + (f) nouns, ex. *Je suis à la gare* (I'm at the station);
à l' + nouns that begin with a vowel, ex. *Je suis à l'aéroport* (I'm at the airport);
aux + plural nouns, ex. *Je vais aux Etats-Unis* (I'm going to the States).

Ceci, cela, ça, (this, that)

"This" is *ceci*, "that" is *cela*, but both are shortened to *ça* in everyday French, ex. *Je voudrais ça* (I'd like this/that).

Celui-ci and *celle-ci* are the (m) and (f) forms for "this one." *Celui-là* and *celle-là* are the (m) and (f) forms for "that one."

Ce, cette, cet, ces (this, that)

Used as an adjective, "this" and "that" are:
ce + (m) nouns, ex. *ce type* (this guy);
cette + (f) nouns, ex. *cette fille* (this girl);
cet + nouns beginning with a vowel, ex. *cet idiot* (that idiot); *ces* + plural nouns,
ex. *ces filles* (those girls).

Adjectives

In French, many adjectives agree with the noun they refer to; this means they change when used with a feminine or plural noun.

Many add an *e* on the end when used with a (f) noun. The *e* also changes the sound of the word as it means you pronounce the consonant, ex. *vert* (green) with a silent *t* becomes *verte* with a voiced *t*:
un pull vert (a green sweater), *une porte verte* (a green door). Most adjectives ending in a vowel add an extra *e* but sound the same, ex. *bleu/bleue*. In this book, adjectives that change are either given twice: (m) form followed by (f) form, ex. *vert/verte* (green), or the (f) form is given in

parentheses after the (m), ex. *vert(e)*.

Some adjectives don't change, ex. any that end in *e* like *sympathique* (nice).

In the plural, most adjectives add an *s*, ex. *des pulls verts* (green sweaters), *des portes vertes* (green doors).

Most adjectives follow the noun but some common ones usually come before, ex.:

beautiful *beau/belle*	young *jeune*
nice, kind *gentil/gentille*	pretty *joli/jolie*
bad *mauvais/mauvaise*	good *bon/bonne*
big, tall *grand/grande*	long *long/longue*
small, short *petit/petite*	old *vieux/vieille*
fat, big *gros/grosse*	

Making comparisons

To make a comparison, put the following words in front of the adjective:
plus (more, ...er), ex. *plus important* (more important), *plus gros* (fatter);
moins (less), ex. *moins gros* (less fat);
aussi (as), ex. *aussi gros* (as fat);
le plus/la plus (the most, the ...est), ex. *le plus important* (the most important).

plus... que (more... than, ...er than), ex. *Il est plus grand que Joe* (He's taller than Joe);
moins... que (less... than), ex. *Elle est moins grande que lui* (She's less tall than him);
aussi... que (as... as), ex. *Il est aussi maigre qu'elle* (He's as thin as her).
Que shortens to *qu'* in front of a vowel.

There are some exceptions, ex. *bon/bonne* (good), *meilleur/meilleure* (better), *le meilleur/la meilleure* (the best), *mauvais/mauvaise* (bad), *pire* (worse), *le pire/la pire* (the worst).

My, your, his, her etc.

These words agree with their noun, ex. *mon frère* (my brother), *ma soeur* (my sister), *mes parents* (my parents).

In front of:	(m) noun	(f) noun	plural noun
my	*mon*	*ma*	*mes*
your	*ton*	*ta*	*tes*
his/her	*son*	*sa*	*ses*
our	*notre*	*notre*	*nos*
your	*votre*	*votre*	*vos*
their	*leur*	*leur*	*leurs*

Before a vowel or *h*, use the (m) form, ex. *mon écharpe* (my scarf) even though *écharpe* is (f).

I, you, he, she etc.

I *je* or *j'*
Je shortens to *j'* in front of vowels, ex. *j'aime* (I like).

you *tu* or *vous*
Say *tu* to a friend, or someone of your own age or younger. Use *vous* when you talk to an adult. If in doubt, use *vous*. *Vous* is also the plural form. Use it when speaking to more than one person.

he *il* she *elle* it *il* or *elle*
There is no special word for "it." Since nouns are (m) or (f), you use "he" to refer to a male or (m) thing and "she" to refer to a female or (f) thing, ex. *Le train? Il est en retard* (The train? It's late) or *La gare? Elle est là-bas* (The station? It's over there.)

we *nous* or *on*
Nous means "we," ex. *Nous sommes en retard* (We are late). However, *nous* sounds formal, so people often use the more colloquial word *on* instead. Like "one" in English, *on* takes the he/she form of the verb: *On est en retard* (We're late)

they *ils* or *elles*
Ils is used for males and (m) things, and *elles* for females and (f) things.

Me, you, him etc.

me *me*	us *nous*	
you *te*	you *vous*	
him/it *le*	her/it *la*	them *les*

In French these come before the verb, ex. *Je le veux* (I want it).

Verbs

French verbs have more tenses (present, future etc.) than English verbs, but there are simple ways of getting by which are explained here.

Present tense

In dictionaries and indexes, verbs are listed in the infinitive form, ex. "to read," "to like". Many French infinitives end in *er* ex. *regarder* (to watch) and follow the same pattern. Drop *er* and replace it with the ending you need:

to watch	*regarder*
I watch	*je regard e*
you watch	*tu regard es*
he/she/it/watches	*il/elle regard e*
we watch	*nous regard ons*
you watch	*vous regard ez*
they watch	*ils/elles regard ent*

French doesn't distinguish between the two English present tenses, ex. "I watch" or "I'm watching," so *je regarde* can mean either. Another tip is that verbs are generally easier than they look: many forms sound the same even though the spelling changes, ex. *aime, aimes* and *aiment* all sound alike.

Useful irregular verbs

to be	être
I am	je suis
you are	tu es
he/she/it is	il/elle est
we are	nous sommes
you are	vous êtes
they are	ils/elles sont
to have (gotten)	avoir
I have	j'ai
you have	tu as
he/she/it has	il/elle a
we have	nous avons
you have	vous avez
they have	ils/elles ont
to go	aller
I go	je vais
you go	tu vas
he/she/it goes	il/elle va
we go	nous allons
you go	vous allez
they go	ils/elles vont
to come	venir
I come	je viens
you come	tu viens
he/she/it comes	il/elle vient
we come	nous venons
you come	vous venez
they come	ils/elles viennent
to make, do	faire
I make, do	je fais
you make, do	tu fais
he/she/it makes, does	il/elle fait
we make, do	nous faisons
you make, do	vous faites
they make, do	ils/elles font

to want (to)	vouloir
I want	je veux
you want	tu veux
he/she/it wants	il/elle veut
we want	nous voulons
you want	vous voulez
they want	ils/elles veulent
to be able to	pouvoir
I can	je peux
you can	tu peux
he/she/it can	il/elle peut
we can	nous pouvons
you can	vous pouvez
they can	ils/elles peuvent
to have to/must	devoir
I have to/must	je dois
you have to/must	tu dois
he/she/it has to/must	il/elle doit
we have to/must	nous devons
you have to/must	vous devez
they have to/must	ils/elles doivent

The last three verbs are handy for making sentences like:
Je veux manger (I want to eat);
Je peux venir avec toi (I can come with you);
Je dois regarder la télé (I must watch TV).
The second verb is in the infinitive (see page 58).

Talking about the future

There is a future tense in French, ex. *Je regarderai la télé* (I shall watch TV) but it is easier to use the "going to" future: *Je vais regarder la télé* (I'm going to watch TV). For everyday use, this form is also more common. As in English, simply use the present of *aller* (to go) + an infinitive (see page 58).

Talking about the past

The easiest way is to use the perfect tense, ex. *J'ai regardé* which can mean "I watched" or "I have watched." You make the perfect with the present of *avoir* (to have) + something called the past participle of the verb:
er verbs change their ending to *é* to make the past participle, ex. *regarder* becomes *regardé* (they sound just the same);
most verbs ending in *ir* in the infinitive change to *i*, ex. *dormir* becomes *dormi*:
il a dormi (he slept/has slept).

Some verbs form the perfect tense with *être* (to be) instead of *avoir*, ex. *Il est allé* (he went/has been). Below are the most useful of these (past participles are also shown if they are not regular *er* or *ir* verbs):

to go *aller*	to stay *rester*
to arrive *arriver*	to come *venir, venu*
to go in *entrer*	to go out *sortir*
to leave *partir*	to go up *monter*
to go home *rentrer*	to fall *tomber*
to go back *retourner*	
to go down *descendre, descendu*	
to become *devenir, devenu*	

The imperfect, or past, tense of "to be" and "to have" is also useful for talking about the past:

I was	*j'étais*
you were	*tu étais*
he/she/it was	*il/elle était*
we were	*nous étions*
you were	*vous étiez*
they were	*ils/elles étaient*

I had	*j'avais*
you had	*tu avais*
he/she/it had	*il/elle avait*
we had	*nous avions*
you had	*vous aviez*
they had	*ils/elles avaient*

Negatives

To make a sentence negative, put *ne* and *pas* on either side of the verb, ex. *je veux* (I want), *je ne veux pas* (I don't want) or *j'aime danser* (I like dancing), *je n'aime pas danser* (I don't like dancing). In spoken French it is common to drop the *ne*, ex. *Je veux pas* (I don't want).

Other useful negative words:
ne... jamais (never), ex.
Il ne veut jamais (He never wants);
ne... personne (nobody), ex.
Je n'aime personne (I don't like anybody);
ne... rien (nothing), ex.
Je ne veux rien (I don't want anything).

Making questions

The simplest way to make a question is to give a sentence the intonation of a question – raise your voice at the end, ex. *Il aime Anne* (He likes Anne) becomes *Il aime Anne?* (Does he like Anne?)
Another way is to put *Est-ce que... ?* at the beginning of the sentence, ex. *Est-ce qu'il aime Anne?* (Does he like Anne?)

In formal, polite French, you change the order of the words, ex. *Voulez-vous du café?* (Would you like some coffee?)

As in English, many questions are formed using a word like *pourquoi* (why?) The question is made in one of the usual ways: with no change to the sentence: *Pourquoi tu veux ça?* (Why do you want that?); with est-ce que: *Pourquoi est-ce que tu veux ça?*; with a change of order: *Pourquoi veux-tu ça?*

These words can be used in the same way:

who? *qui?*	where? *où?*
what *quoi?*	when? *quand?*
which? *quel?*	how? *comment?*
how much? *combien?*	

Word list

This list gives you some useful words that will help you get by in French. Adjectives with two forms are given twice: (m) followed by (f) (see page 57) and verbs are given in the infinitive.

accident	l'accident (m)
address	l'adresse (f)
in advance	à l'avance
after	après
afternoon	l'après-midi (f)
against	contre
age	l'âge (m)
to agree	être d'accord
airplane	l'avion (f)
airport	l'aéroport (m)
alone	seul/seule
ambulance	l'ambulance (f)
and	et
another	un/une autre
anyone, someone	quelqu'un
appetizer	l'entrée (f)
to arrive	arriver
to ask	demander
bad	mauvais/mauvaise
bag	le sac
bakery	la boulangerie
ball	le ballon, la balle
bank	la banque
bathtub	le bain
bathroom	la salle de bain
to be	être
beach	la plage
beautiful	beau/belle
because	parce que
behind	derrière
to believe	croire
beware	attention
bicycle	le vélo
big	gros/grosse, grand/grande
bill	l'addition (f)
bill (money)	le billet
birthday	l'anniversaire (m)
boat	le bateau
book	le livre, le bouquin*
to book, reserve	réserver
booking	la réservation
boring	ennuyeux/ennuyeuse
to borrow	emprunter
bottle	la bouteille
boy	le garçon
bread	le pain
to break	casser
to break down	tomber en panne
breakfast	le petit déjeuner
bridge	le pont
brother	le frère
bus	le bus, l'autobus

bus station	la gare routière
bus stop	l'arrêt d'autobus (m)
busy	prise/prise
but	mais
butter	le beurre
to buy	acheter
bye	salut
café	le café, le bar
cake	le gâteau
to call	appeler
to camp	camper
camping	le camping
to cancel	annuler
car	la voiture, la bagnole*
to carry	porter
cashier's desk	la caisse
castle	le château
to catch	attraper
cathedral	la cathédrale
chair	le chaise
to change	changer
cheap	pas cher/pas chère
cheese	le fromage
chocolate	le chocolat
church	l'église (f)
close (to)	près (de)
closed	fermé/fermée
clothes	les vêtements (m pl)
coffee	le café
cold	froid/froide
color	la couleur
to come	venir
completely	complètement
to confirm	confirmer
cool	cool*, super*
to cost	coûter
countryside	la campagne
to cross	traverser
crossroads	le carrefour
customs	la douane
dangerous	dangereux/dangereuse
day	le jour
delay	le retard
delicious	délicieux/délicieuse
department store	le grand magasin
dessert	le dessert
dictionary	le dictionnaire
difficult	difficile
dinner	le dîner
to do	faire
doctor	le médecin
downstairs	en bas
drink	la boisson
to drink	boire
drinking water	l'eau potable (f)
easy	facile
to eat	manger
egg	l'oeuf (m)

61

end of, at the end of	*au bout de*	key	*le clé*
English	*l'anglais (m)*	kind (type)	*le genre*
enough	*assez*	knife	*le couteau*
entrance	*l'entrée (f)*	to know	*savoir, connaître*
evening	*le soir*		
every day	*tous les jours*	large	*grand/grande*
except	*sauf*	last	*le dernier*
excuse me	*pardon, s'il vous plaît*	later	*plus tard*
exit	*la sortie*	latest	*dernier/dernière*
to expect	*s'attendre à, prévoir*	to learn	*apprendre*
expensive	*cher/chère*	to leave	*laisser*
to explain	*expliquer*	to leave (depart)	*partir*
		left	*à gauche*
fairly	*assez*	lemon	*le citron*
family	*la famille*	less	*moins*
far	*loin*	library	*la bibliothèque*
father	*le père*	to like	*aimer*
to finish	*finir*	to listen	*écouter*
first	*le premier/la première*	a little	*un petit peu, un peu*
fish	*le poisson*	to live	*habiter*
fork	*la fourchette*	long	*long/longue*
French	*le français*	to look	*regarder*
friend	*l'ami/l'amie*	to look for	*chercher*
fruit	*les fruits (m pl)*	to lose	*perdre*
full	*complet/complète*	lost	*perdu/perdue*
		loud	*fort/forte*
girl	*la fille*	lunch	*le déjeuner*
glass	*le verre*		
glasses	*les lunettes (f pl)*	Madam, Mrs.	*Madame*
to go	*aller*	mailbox	*la boîte aux lettres*
good	*bon/bonne*	main course	*le plat principal*
goodbye	*au revoir*	makeup	*du maquillage (m)*
great	*génial/géniale*	man	*l'homme (m)*
guide book	*le guide*	map	*le plan, la carte*
		market	*le marché*
hair	*les cheveux (m pl)*	maybe	*peut-être*
happy	*heureux/heureuse*	meal	*le repas*
to have	*avoir*	meat	*la viande*
to hear	*écouter*	medicine	*le médicament*
heavy	*lourd/lourde*	to meet	*rencontrer, se retrouver*
hello	*bonjour*	menu	*la carte, le menu*
to help	*aider*	milk	*le lait*
here	*ici*	mineral water	*l'eau minérale (f)*
Hi!	*Salut!*	Miss	*Mademoiselle*
hospital	*l'hôpital (m)*	money	*l'argent (m)*
hot	*chaud/chaude*	month	*le mois*
hotel	*l'hôtel (m)*	more	*plus*
house	*la maison*	morning	*le matin*
How?	*Comment?*	mother	*la mère*
(to be) hungry	*(avoir) faim*	Mr., Sir	*Monsieur*
husband	*le mari*	Mrs., Madam	*Madame*
		museum	*le musée*
important	*important/importante*	music	*la musique*
ill	*malade*		
in front of	*devant*	name	*le nom*
interesting	*intéressant/intéressante*	last	*le nom de famille*
		narrow	*étroit*
jacket	*la veste*	near (to)	*près (de)*
jam	*la confiture*	nearby	*tout près, juste à côté*
job	*le boulot*	new	*nouveau/nouvelle*
journey	*le voyage*	news	*les informations (f pl)*

newspaper	le journal (pl les journaux)	sad	triste
next	le prochain/la prochaine	salad	la salade
		salt	le sel
nice	gentil/gentille	to say	dire
nice (OK)	sympa	schedule	l'horaire (m)
night	la nuit	school	l'école (f)
no	non	sea	la mer
now	maintenant	seat	la place
number	le nombre	to see	voir
		to see again	se revoir
		see you soon	à bientôt
OK	bien	to sell	vendre
old	vieux/vieille	shampoo	le shampooing
one way	sens unique	short	court/courte, petit/petite
open	ouvert/ouverte	to show	montrer
opposite	en face de	shower (bathroom)	la douche
or	ou	to be sick	vomir
to order	commander	to sing	chanter
other	autre	sister	la soeur
outdoor	en plein air	size	la taille
over	par dessus	to sleep	dormir
		small	petit/petite
passport	le passeport	snow	la neige
(in) the past	(dans) le passé	so	tellement
pasta	les pâtes (f pl)	soap	le savon
to pay	payer	someone	quelqu'un
people	les gens (m pl)	something	quelque chose
pepper	le poivre	song	la chanson
pharmacy	la pharmacie	sorry	désolé/désolée
phone	le téléphone	soup	la soupe, le potage
picnic	le pique-nique	to speak	parler
plate	l'assiette	spoon	la cuillère
platform	le quai	square	la place, le square
to play	jouer	stairs	l'escalier (m)
please	s'il vous plaît, s'il te plaît	stamp	le timbre
		to start	commencer
police	la police	(train) station	la gare
postcard	la carte postale	to stay	rester
post office	la poste	store	le magasin
to prefer	préférer	straight ahead	tout droit
pretty	joli/jolie	street	la rue, le boulevard
price	le prix	strong	fort/forte
to put	mettre	student	l'étudiant/l'étudiante
		to study	étudier
radio	la radio	sugar	le sucre
rain	la pluie	sun	le soleil
to read	lire	sunglasses	les lunettes de soleil (f pl)
really	vraiment	sunscreen	l'écran total
to rent	louer	supermarket	le supermarché
to repeat	répéter	sweet (taste)	sucré/sucrée
to reserve	réserver	to swim	se baigner, nager
restaurant	le restaurant, le resto*	swimming pool	la piscine
right	à droite		
to be right	avoir raison	table	la table
river	la rivière	to take	prendre
road	la route	tall	grand/grande
room	la chambre	taxi	le taxi
rose	la rose	tea	le thé
rude	grossier/grossière	teacher	le professeur/la prof*
rules	les règles	telephone	le téléphone
to run	courir	to tell	dire

TV	*la télé*	to use	*utiliser*
thank you	*merci*		
there	*là*	very	*très*
things	*les affaires (f pl), les trucs**	village	*le village*
to think	*penser*	to wake up	*se réveiller*
to think about	*réfléchir*	to walk	*marcher*
(to be) thirsty	*(avoir) soif*	to want	*vouloir*
ticket	*le billet, le ticket*	to wash	*laver*
time	*le temps*	water	*l'eau (f)*
tired	*fatigué/fatiguée*	to wear (clothes)	*porter*
tissue	*le mouchoir en papier*	weather	*le temps*
today	*aujourd'hui*	week	*la semaine*
toilet	*les toilettes (f pl)*	weird	*bizarre*
tomorrow	*demain*	What?	*Quoi?*
tonight	*ce soir*	when	*quand*
too	*trop, aussi*	where	*où*
town	*la ville*	why	*pourquoi*
town hall	*la mairie, l'hôtel de ville (m)*	with	*avec*
		woman	*la femme*
train	*le train*	work	*le travail*
to try, to try on	*essayer*	to write	*écrire*
to turn	*tourner*		
		year	*l'an (m), l'année (f)*
under	*en dessous*	yes	*oui*
to understand	*comprendre*	yesterday	*hier*

Index

If you can't find the phrasebook section you want from the Contents page, try looking here.